"Your book brought tears and laughter.

— Dr. Ines Freedman
Sunnyvale, California

"Your book made a deep impression on me…I felt as though someone had just slapped my face and woke me up."

— Alan Kaplan
aikido teacher

"Hard to find words to explain the experience. It helped me find an inner peace stronger than I've ever known."

— Sue Tabashnik
Southfield, Michigan

"My young students loved your book…because they were able to apply the lessons in life."

— Dennis Edwards
West British Columbia

"My name is Hope. I'm fifteen years old. Your book changed my life."

— Hope Wagner
Hinkley, Ohio

"Is it true? Maybe, maybe not…but it's totally true in its ability to make you reflect on the deepest questions of life."

— Charles Tart, PhD
professor of psychology

"Your book has helped me experience feelings I haven't felt since I was a very young child. I'm renewed with the pleasures of just being alive."

— Deb Paschal
San Diego, California

Books by Dan Millman

THE PEACEFUL WARRIOR SAGA
Way of the Peaceful Warrior
Sacred Journey of the Peaceful Warrior
The Journeys of Socrates

GUIDEBOOKS
The Life You Were Born to Live
Everyday Enlightenment
No Ordinary Moments
The Laws of Spirit
Body Mind Mastery
Living on Purpose

CHILDREN'S BOOKS
Secret of the Peaceful Warrior
Quest for the Crystal Castle

WAY OF THE

PEACEFUL WARRIOR

WAY OF THE
PEACEFUL WARRIOR

A BOOK THAT CHANGES LIVES

DAN MILLMAN

H J KRAMER

NEW WORLD LIBRARY
NOVATO, CALIFORNIA

An H J Kramer Book
published in a joint venture with
New World Library

Editorial office: Administrative office:
H J Kramer Inc.   New World Library
P.O. Box 1082   14 Pamaron Way
Tiburon, California 94920   Novato, California 94949

Design and composition: Tona Pearce Myers

Library of Congress Cataloging-in-Publication Data

Millman, Dan.
Way of the peaceful warrior : a book that changes lives / Dan
Millman.
p. cm.
ISBN-10: 1-932073-20-5 (alk. paper)
1. Spiritual life. 2. Millman, Dan. I. Title.
BL624.M533 2000
291.4'4—dc21   00-055922

First printing movie tie-in edition, June 2006
Movie edition ISBN-13: 978-1-932073-20-1
Classic edition ISBN-10: 0-915811-89-8
Printed in Canada on acid-free paper

10 9 8 7 6 5 4

*To the Ultimate Warrior of Peace,
of whom Socrates is but
a twinkling reflection —
Who has no name yet many,
and Who is the Source of us all.*

CONTENTS

ACKNOWLEDGMENTS

L ife has blessed me with many teachers and guiding influences who have, in their own ways, each contributed to
the writing of this book. Not least among them are my parents, Herman and Vivian Millman, who nourished me with
their love, faith, and sacrifice, and my publisher, Hal Kramer,
who trusted his inner light and keen publishing instincts to
take a chance on this book. Thanks also to copublisher Linda
Kramer, for her unsparing support and passionate integrity,
and to Marc Allen, Jason Gardner, and the team at New
World Library, whose sage publishing wisdom has created a
vibrant launching pad for my book in its twentieth year and
beyond.

From the start, Charlie Winton and the staff at Publishers
Group West provided an instrumental link between author,
publisher, and the public. Their excellent work too often goes
unheralded, but their efforts are key for many authors and
are much appreciated by this one. Thanks also to my agents
Michael Larsen and Elizabeth Pomada.

And last, but always first, my abiding love and gratitude
to Joy — my wife, companion, friend, teacher, toughest
editor, and most loyal supporter — a blessing in my life and
a guardian angel for my spirit.

And, of course, there's Soc.

PREFACE

A n extraordinary series of events took place in my life, beginning in December 1966, during my junior year at the University of California at Berkeley. It all began at 3:20 A.M., when I first stumbled upon Socrates in an all-night gas station. (He didn't volunteer his real name, but after spending time with him that first night, I named him on impulse after the ancient Greek sage; he liked the name, so it stuck.) That chance encounter and the adventures that followed were to transform my life.

The years prior to 1966 had smiled upon me. Raised by loving parents in a secure environment, I was later to win the World Trampoline Championship in London, travel through Europe, and receive many honors. Life brought rewards, but no lasting peace or satisfaction.

Now I realize that I had, in a sense, been sleeping all those years and just dreaming I was awake — until I met Socrates, who came to be my mentor and friend. Before that time, I'd always believed that a life of quality, enjoyment, and wisdom were my human birthright and would be automatically bestowed upon me as time passed. I never suspected that I would have to learn *how* to live — that there were specific disciplines and ways of seeing the world I had to master before I could awaken to a simple, happy, uncomplicated life.

Socrates showed me the error of my ways by contrasting them with *his* way, the Way of the Peaceful Warrior. He constantly poked fun at my own serious, concerned, problematic life, until I came to see through his eyes of wisdom, compassion, and humor. And he never let up until I discovered what it means to live as a warrior.

Often I sat with him far into the early morning hours — listening to him, arguing with him, and, in spite of myself, laughing with him. This story is based on my adventure, but it *is* a novel. The man I called Socrates did, in fact, exist. Yet he had a way of blending into the world, so it's been difficult at times to tell where he left off and other teachers and life experiences began. I have taken liberties with the dialogue and with some time sequences and have sprinkled anecdotes and metaphors into the story to highlight the lessons Socrates would want me to convey.

Life is not a private affair. A story and its lessons are only made useful if shared. So I've chosen to honor my teacher by sharing his piercing wisdom and humor with you.

WAY OF THE
PEACEFUL WARRIOR

Warriors, warriors we call ourselves.
We fight for splendid virtue, for high endeavor, for
sublime wisdom, therefore we call ourselves warriors.

— Aunguttara Nikaya

THE GAS STATION
AT RAINBOW'S END

L ife begins," I thought, as I waved good-bye to Mom and
Dad and pulled away from the curb in my reliable old
Valiant, its faded white body stuffed with the belongings I'd
packed for my first year at college. I felt strong, independent,
ready for anything.

Singing to myself above the radio's music, I sped north
across the freeways of Los Angeles, then up and over the
Grapevine, connecting with Route 99, which carried me
through the green agricultural flatlands stretching to the foot
of the San Gabriel Mountains.

Just before dusk, my winding descent through the Oakland
hills brought me a shimmering view of San Francisco Bay. My
excitement grew as I neared the Berkeley campus.

After finding my dormitory, I unpacked and gazed out the
window at the Golden Gate Bridge and the lights of San
Francisco sparkling in the darkness.

Five minutes later I was walking along Telegraph Avenue,
looking in shop windows, breathing the fresh northern
California air, savoring the smells drifting out of tiny cafés.
Overwhelmed by it all, I walked the beautifully landscaped
paths of the campus until after midnight.

The next morning, immediately after breakfast, I walked

3

down to Harmon Gymnasium, where I'd be training six days a week, four muscle-straining, somersaulting, sweaty hours each day, pursuing my dreams of becoming a champion.

Two days passed, and I was already drowning in a sea of people, papers, and class schedules. Soon the months blended together, passing and changing softly, like the mild California seasons. In my classes I survived; in the gym, I thrived. A friend once told me I was born to be an acrobat. I certainly looked the part: clean cut, short brown hair, a lean, wiry body. I'd always had a penchant for daredevil stunts; even as a child I enjoyed playing on the edge of fear. The gymnastics room had become my sanctuary, where I found excitement, challenge, and a measure of satisfaction.

By the end of my first two years I had flown to Germany, France, and England, representing the United States Gymnastics Federation. I won the World Trampoline Championship; my gymnastics trophies were piling up in the corner of my room; my picture appeared in the *Daily Californian* with such regularity that people began to recognize me and my reputation grew. Women smiled at me. Susie, a savory, unfailingly sweet friend with short blond hair and a toothpaste smile, paid me amorous visits more and more often. Even my studies were going well. I felt on top of the world.

However, in the early autumn of 1966, my junior year, something dark and intangible began to take shape. By then I'd moved out of the dorm and was living alone in a small studio behind my landlord's house. During this time I felt a growing melancholy, even in the midst of all my achievements. Shortly thereafter, the nightmares started. Nearly every night I jerked awake, sweating. Almost always, the dream was the same:

> I *walk along a dark city street; tall buildings without doors or windows loom at me through a dark swirling mist.*
>
> A *towering shape cloaked in black strides toward*

me. I feel rather than see a chilling specter, a gleaming white skull with black eye sockets that stare at me in deathly silence. A finger of white bone points at me; the white knucklebones curl into a beckoning claw. I freeze.

A white-haired man appears from behind the hooded terror; his face is calm and unlined. His footsteps make no sound. I sense somehow, that he is my only hope of escape; he has the power to save me, but he doesn't see me and I can't call to him.

Mocking my fear, the black-hooded Death whirls around to face the white-haired man, who laughs in his face. Stunned, I watch. Death furiously makes a grab for him. The next moment the specter is hurtling toward me, as the old man seizes him by his cloak and tosses him into the air.

Suddenly the Grim Reaper vanishes. The man with the shining white hair looks at me and holds out his hands in a gesture of welcome. I walk toward him, then directly into him, dissolving into his body. When I look down at myself, I see that I'm wearing a black robe. I raise my hands and see bleached white, gnarled bones, come together in prayer.

I'd awake with a gasp.

One night, early in December, I lay in bed listening to the howling wind driving through a small crack in the window of my apartment. Sleepless, I got up and threw on my faded Levi's, a T-shirt, sneakers, and down jacket, and walked out into the night. It was 3:05 A.M.

I walked aimlessly, inhaling deeply the moist, chilly air, looking up into the starlit sky, listening for a rare sound in the silent streets. The cold made me hungry, so I headed for an all-night gas station to buy some cookies and a soft drink. Hands in my pockets, I hurried across campus, past sleeping houses, before I came to the lights of the service station. It was a bright fluorescent oasis in a darkened wilderness of closed food joints, shops, and movie theaters.

I rounded the corner of the garage adjoining the station and nearly fell over a man sitting in the shadows, leaning his chair back against the red tile station wall. Startled, I retreated. He was wearing a red wool cap, gray corduroy pants, white socks, and Japanese sandals. He seemed comfortable enough in a light windbreaker though the wall thermometer by his head registered 38 degrees.

Without looking up, he said in a strong, almost musical voice, "Sorry if I frightened you."

"Oh, uh, that's OK. Do you have any soda pop?"

"Only have fruit juice here. And don't call me 'Pop'!" He turned toward me and with a half smile removed his cap, revealing shining white hair. Then he laughed.

That laugh! I stared blankly at him for one more moment. He was the old man in my dream! The white hair, the clear, unlined face, a tall slim man of fifty or sixty. He laughed again. In my confusion I somehow found my way to the door marked "Office" and pushed it open. Along with the office door, I had felt another door opening to another dimension. I collapsed onto an old couch and shivered, wondering what might come screaming through that door into my orderly world. My dread was mixed with a strange fascination that I couldn't fathom. I sat, breathing shallowly, trying to regain my previous hold on the ordinary world.

I looked around the office. It was so different from the sterility and disarray of the usual gas station. The couch I was sitting on was covered by a faded but colorful Mexican blanket. To my left, near the entryway, stood a case of neatly organized traveler's aids: maps, fuses, sunglasses, and so on. Behind a small, dark brown walnut desk was an earth-colored, corduroy-upholstered chair. A springwater dispenser guarded a door marked "Private." Near me was a second door that led to the garage.

What struck me most of all was the homelike atmosphere of the room. A bright yellow shag rug ran its length, stopping just short of the welcome mat at the entry. The walls had recently been painted white, and a few landscape paintings lent them color. The soft incandescent glow of the lights calmed me. It was a relaxing contrast to the fluorescent glare outside. Overall, the room felt warm, orderly, and secure.

How could I have known that it was to be a place of unpredictable adventure, magic, terror, and romance? I only thought then, A fireplace would fit in nicely here.

Soon my breathing had relaxed, and my mind, if not content, had at least stopped whirling. This white-haired man's resemblance to the man in my dream was surely a coincidence. With a sigh, I stood, zipped up my jacket, and sallied forth in the chill air.

He was still sitting there. As I walked past and stole a last quick look at his face, a glimmer in his eyes caught mine. His eyes were like none I'd seen before. At first they seemed to have tears in them, ready to spill over; then the tears turned to a twinkle, like a reflection of the starlight. I was drawn deeper into his gaze until the stars themselves became only a reflection of his eyes. I was lost for a time, seeing nothing but those eyes, the unyielding and curious eyes of an infant.

I don't know how long I stood there; it could have been seconds or minutes — maybe longer. With a start, I became aware of where I was. Mumbling a good night, feeling off balance, I hurried toward the corner.

When I reached the curb, I stopped. My neck tingled; I felt that he was watching me. I glanced back. No more than fifteen seconds had passed. But there he was, *standing on the roof,* his arms crossed, looking up at the starry sky. I gaped at the empty chair still leaning back against the wall, then up again. It was impossible! If he had been changing a wheel on a carriage made from a giant pumpkin drawn by huge mice, the effect couldn't have been any more startling.

In the stillness of the night, I stared up at his lean shape, an imposing presence even at a distance. I heard the stars chime like bells singing in the wind. Suddenly he snapped his head around and stared directly into my eyes. He was about sixty feet away, but I could almost feel his breath on my face. I shivered, but not from the cold. That doorway, where reality dissolved into dreams, cracked open again.

I looked up at him. "Yes?" he said. "Can I help you?" Prophetic words!

"Excuse me, but..."

"You are excused," he smiled. I felt my face flush; this was starting to irritate me. He was playing a game with me, but I didn't know the rules.

"All right, how did you get up on the roof?"

"Get up on the roof?" he queried, looking innocent and puzzled.

"Yes. How did you get from that chair," I pointed, "up to that roof, in less than twenty seconds? You were leaning back against the wall, right there. I turned, walked over to the corner, and you..."

"I know exactly what *I* was doing," his voice boomed. "There is no need to describe it to me. The question is, do you know what *you* were doing?"

"Of course I know what I was doing!" I was getting angry now; I wasn't some child to be lectured to! But I desperately wanted to find out the old man's gimmick, so I held my temper and requested politely, "Please, sir, tell me how you got up on the roof."

He just stared down at me in silence until the back of my neck began to get prickly. Finally he replied, "Used a ladder. It's around back." Then, ignoring me, he looked upward again.

I walked quickly around back. Sure enough, there was an old ladder leaning crookedly against the back wall. But the ladder's top was at least five feet short of the roof's edge; even if he could have used it — which was highly doubtful — that wouldn't explain how he got up there in a few seconds.

Something landed on my shoulder in the darkness. I gasped, and whirled around to see his hand. Somehow he'd gotten *off* the roof and crept up on me. Then I guessed the only possible answer. He had a twin. They obviously got their kicks scaring the wits out of innocent visitors. I accused him immediately.

"All right, mister, where's your twin? I'm nobody's fool."

He frowned slightly, then started to roar with laughter. Hah! That clinched it. I was right; I'd found him out. But his answer made me less sure of myself.

"If I had a twin, do you think I'd be the one wasting my time standing here talking with 'nobody's fool'?" He laughed again and strode back toward the garage, leaving me standing openmouthed. I couldn't believe the nerve of this guy.

I hurried to catch up with him. He walked into the garage and started to tinker with a carburetor under the hood of an old green Ford pickup. "So you think I'm a fool?" I said, sounding more belligerent than I'd intended.

"We're all fools together," he replied. "It's just that a few people know it; others don't. You seem to be one of the latter types. Hand me that small wrench, will you?"

I handed him his damn wrench and started to leave. Before I left, though, I had to know. "Would you please tell me how you got up to the roof so fast? I'm really puzzled."

He handed me back the wrench, saying, "The world's a puzzle; no need to make sense out of it." He pointed to the shelf behind me. "I'll need the hammer and the screwdriver now, over there."

Frustrated, I watched him for another minute, trying to figure out how to get him to tell me what I wanted to know, but he seemed oblivious to my presence.

I gave up and started toward the door, when I heard him say, "Stick around and make yourself useful." Deftly removing the carburetor like a surgeon in the middle of a heart transplant, he set it down carefully and turned to face me. "Here," he said, handing me the carburetor. "Take this apart and put the pieces in that can to soak. It will take your mind off your questions."

My frustration dissolved into laughter. This old man could be irritating, but he was interesting, too. I decided to be sociable.

"My name's Dan," I said, reaching out to shake his hand, smiling insincerely. "What's yours?"

He placed a screwdriver in my outstretched hand. "My name doesn't matter; neither does yours. What *is* important is what lies beyond names and beyond questions. Now, you will need this screwdriver to take apart that carburetor," he pointed.

"Nothing lies beyond questions," I retorted. "Like how did you fly up on that rooftop?"

"I didn't fly — I jumped," was his poker-faced reply. "It's not magic, so don't get your hopes up. In your case, however, I may have to perform some very difficult magic. It looks as if I'm going to have to transform a jackass into a human being."

"Who the hell do you think you are?"

"I am a warrior!" he snapped. "Beyond that, who I am depends on who you *want* me to be."

"Can't you just answer a straight question?" I attacked the carburetor with a vengeance.

"Ask me one and I'll try," he said, smiling innocently. The screwdriver slipped and I skinned my finger. "Damn!" I yelled, going to the sink to wash the cut. He handed me a Band-Aid.

"All right then. Here is a straight question." I determined to keep my voice patient. "How can you be useful to me?"

"I have already been useful to you," he replied, pointing to the bandage on my finger.

That did it. "Look, I can't waste my time here any longer. I need to get some sleep." I put the carburetor down and got ready to leave.

"How do you know you haven't been asleep your whole

life? How do you know you're not asleep right now?" he said, watching me intently.

"Whatever you say." I was too tired to argue. "One thing, though. Before I go, how did you pull off that stunt — you know, on the — ?"

"Tomorrow, Dan, tomorrow," he interrupted. Then he smiled warmly, and all my fears and frustration dissolved. He reached out and clasped my bandaged hand. Soon my hand, my arm, then my whole body started to tingle. He added, "It's been pleasant seeing you again."

"What do you mean 'again'?" I began, then caught myself; "I know, tomorrow, tomorrow." We both laughed. I walked to the door, stopped, turned, stared at him, then said, "Good-bye — *Socrates*."

He looked bewildered, then shrugged good-naturedly. I think he liked the name. I left without another word.

I slept through my eight o'clock class the next morning. By the time my afternoon gymnastics workout started, I was awake and ready to go.

After running up and down the bleacher stairs, Rick, Sid, and I, along with our teammates, lay on the floor, sweating and panting, stretching our legs, shoulders, and backs. Usually I was silent during this ritual, but today I felt like telling them about last night. All I could say was, "I met this unusual guy at a gas station last night."

My friends were more involved with the stretching pain in their legs than in my little story.

We warmed up easily, doing a few handstand push-ups, some sit-ups, and leg raises, and then began our tumbling series. As I flew through the air again and again — as I swung around the high bar, did scissors on the pommel horse, and struggled through a new muscle-straining ring routine — I wondered about the mysterious feats of the man I'd named Socrates. My ruffled feelings urged me to avoid him, but I had to make sense out of this enigmatic character.

After dinner, I quickly read through my history and psychology assignments, wrote a rough draft of an English paper, and raced out of the apartment. It was 11:00 P.M. Doubts began to plague me as I neared the station. Did he really want to see me again? What could I say to impress upon him the fact that I was a highly intelligent person?

He was there, standing in the doorway. He bowed, and with a wave of his arm welcomed me into his office. "Please, remove your shoes — a custom of mine."

I sat down on the couch and put my shoes nearby, in case I wanted to make a hasty exit. I still didn't trust this mysterious stranger.

It was starting to rain outside. The color and warmth of the office was a comfortable contrast to the dark night and ominous clouds outside. I started to feel at ease. Leaning back, I said, "You know, Socrates, I feel as though I've met you before."

"You have," he answered, again opening the doorway in my mind where dreams and reality become one. I paused.

"Uh, Socrates, I've been having this dream — you're in it." I watched him carefully, but his face revealed nothing.

"I've been in many people's dreams; so have you. Tell me about your dream," he smiled.

I told him, in as much detail as I could remember. The room seemed to darken as the terrible scenes became vivid in my mind, and my familiar world began to recede.

After I finished, he said, "Yes, a very good dream." Before I could ask him what he meant by that, the station bell clanged, and clanged again. He put on a poncho and went outside into the wet night. I stared out the window, watching him.

It was a busy time of evening: the Friday-night rush. Things got pretty hectic, with one customer driving in after another. I felt silly just sitting there so I went out to help him, but he didn't seem to notice me.

An endless line of cars greeted me: two-tones, reds, greens, blacks, hardtops, pickups, and foreign sports cars. The moods of the customers varied as much as their cars. Only one or two people seemed to know Socrates, but many people looked twice at him, as if noticing something odd but indefinable.

Some of the people were in a party mood, laughing loudly and blaring their radios while we waited on them. Socrates laughed right along with them. One or two customers were sullen, putting forth a special effort to be unpleasant, but Socrates treated one and all with the same courtesy — as if each person were his personal guest.

After midnight, the cars and customers grew scarce. The cool air seemed unnaturally still after having been filled with raucous noise and activity. As we entered the office, Socrates thanked me for my assistance. I shrugged it off but was pleased that he'd noticed. It had been a long time since I'd helped anyone with anything.

Once inside the warm office, I remembered our unfinished business. I started talking as soon as I flopped onto the couch. "Socrates, I have a couple of questions."

He held his hands in a gesture of prayer, looking upward to the office ceiling as if asking for divine guidance — or divine patience. "What," he said with a sigh, "are your questions?"

"Well, I still want to know about the roof, and why you said, 'I'm pleased to see you *again*,' and I want to know what I can do for you and how you can be useful to me. *And,* I want to know how old you are."

"Let's take the easiest one, for now. I'm ninety-six years old, by your time." He was not ninety-six. Fifty-six, maybe; sixty-six at the outside; seventy-six, possible but amazing. But *ninety-six?* He was lying — but why would he lie? And I had to find out about the other thing he had let slip, too.

"Socrates, what do you mean 'by your time'? Are you on eastern standard time or are you," I joked feebly, "from outer space?"

"Isn't everyone?" he replied. By then, I had already considered that as a distinct possibility.

"I still want to know what we can do for each other."

"Just this: I wouldn't mind having one last student, and you obviously need a teacher."

"I have enough teachers," I said too quickly.

He paused and drew a deep breath. "Whether you have a proper teacher or not depends upon what you want to learn." He rose lightly from his chair and walked to the door. "Come with me. I want to show you something."

We walked to the corner, from where we could see down the avenue to the lights of the business district and beyond them to the lights of San Francisco.

"The world out there," he said, waving his arm across the horizon, "is a school, Dan. Life is the only real teacher. It offers many experiences, and if experience alone brought wisdom and fulfillment, then elderly people would all be happy, enlightened masters. But the lessons of experience are hidden. I can help you learn from experience to see the world clearly, and clarity is something you desperately need right now. You know this is true, but your mind rebels; you haven't yet turned knowledge into wisdom."

"I don't know about that — I mean, I wouldn't go that far."

"No, Dan, you don't know about it yet, but you will go that far and beyond."

We headed back for the office just as a shiny red Toyota pulled in. Socrates continued talking as he opened the gas tank. "Like most people, you've been taught to gather information from outside yourself, from books, magazines, experts." He stuck the gas nozzle into the tank. "Like this car, you open up and let the facts pour in. Sometimes the information is premium and sometimes it's low octane. You buy your knowledge at the current market rates, much like you buy gasoline."

"Hey, thanks for reminding me. My tuition check for next quarter is due in two days."

Socrates just nodded and continued to fill the customer's tank. When the tank was full, Socrates kept pumping gas, until

14

fuel started overflowing the tank and pouring down onto the ground. A flood of gasoline ran across the pavement.

"Socrates! The tank is full — watch what you're doing!"

Ignoring me, he let the flood continue — saying, "Dan, like this gas tank, you are overflowing with preconceptions, full of useless knowledge. You hold many facts and opinions, yet know little of yourself. Before you can learn, you'll have to first empty your tank." He grinned at me, winked, and turning the pump off with a click, added, "Clean up the mess, will you?"

I got the feeling he was referring to more than the spilled gas. I hurriedly watered down the pavement. Soc took the driver's money and gave him back some change and a smile. We walked back to the office and settled in.

"What are you going to do, fill me full of *your* facts?" I bristled.

"It's not a matter of facts; it's a matter of body wisdom."

"What's 'body wisdom'?"

"Everything you'll ever need to know is within you; the secrets of the universe are imprinted on the cells of your body. But you haven't learned how to read the wisdom of the body. So you can only read books and listen to experts and hope they are right."

I couldn't believe it — this gas station attendant was accusing my professors of ignorance and implying that my college education was pointless. "I understand this 'body wisdom' concept, but I don't buy it."

He shook his head slowly. "You understand many things but have realized practically nothing."

"What is that supposed to mean?"

"Understanding is the one-dimensional comprehension of the intellect. It leads to knowledge. Realization is three-dimensional — a simultaneous comprehension of head, heart, and instinct. It comes only from direct experience."

"I'm still not with you."

"Do you remember when you first learned to drive? Prior to that time, you'd been a passenger; you only understood

15

what it was. But you *realized* what it was like when you did it for the first time."

"That's right!" I said. "I remember feeling, So that's what it's like!"

"Exactly! That phrase describes the experience of realization perfectly. One day, you'll say the same thing about life."

I sat quietly for a moment, then piped up. "You still haven't explained how body wisdom works."

"Come with me," Socrates beckoned, leading me toward the door marked "Private." Once inside, we were in total darkness. I started to tense, but then the fear gave way to keen anticipation. I was about to learn my first real secret: body wisdom.

The lights flashed on. We were in a bathroom and Socrates was peeing loudly into the toilet bowl. "Ahh," he said, "now *this* is body wisdom!" His laughter echoed off the tile walls as I stomped out, sat on the couch, and glared at the rug.

When he emerged, I said, "Socrates, I still want to know..."

"If you are going to call me 'Socrates,'" he interrupted, "you might at least do the name honor by allowing me to ask the questions on occasion, and you can answer them. How does that sound?"

"Fine!" I responded. "You just asked your question, and I answered it. Now it's my turn. About that flying stunt you pulled the other night..."

"You are a persistent young man, aren't you?"

"Yes, I am. I didn't get where I am today without persistence. And that's another question I've answered. Now, can we deal with some of mine?"

Ignoring me, he asked, "Where are you today, right now?"

Eagerly, I started talking about myself. However, I noticed that I was being sidetracked from getting answers to my questions. Still, I told him about my distant and recent past and about my inexplicable depressions. He listened patiently and intently, as if he had all the time in the world, until I finished several hours later.

"Very well," he said. "But you still have not answered my question about where you are."

"Yes I did, remember? I told you how I got to where I am today: by hard work."

"Where are you?"

"What do you mean, where am I?"

"Where *are* you?" he repeated softly.

"I'm here."

"Where is here?"

"In this office, in this gas station!" I was getting impatient with this game.

"Where is this gas station?"

"In Berkeley?"

"Where is Berkeley?"

"In California?"

"Where is California?"

"In the United States?"

"Where is the United States?"

"On a landmass, one of the continents in the Western Hemisphere. Socrates, I..."

"Where are the continents?"

I sighed. "On the earth. Are we done yet?"

"Where is the earth?"

"In the solar system, third planet from the sun. The sun is a small star in the Milky Way galaxy, all right?"

"Where is the Milky Way?"

"Oh, brother," I sighed impatiently, rolling my eyes. "In the universe." I sat back and crossed my arms with finality.

"And where," Socrates smiled, "is the universe?"

"The universe is, well, there are theories about how it's shaped..."

"That's not what I asked. Where is it?"

"I don't know — how can I answer that?"

"That is the point. You cannot answer it, and you never will. There is no knowing about it. You are ignorant of where

17

the universe is, and thus, where you are. In fact, you have no knowledge of where anything is or of *what* anything is or how it came to be. Life is a mystery.

"My ignorance is based on this understanding. Your understanding is based on ignorance. This is why I am a humorous fool, and you are a serious jackass."

"Listen!" I said. "There are things you should know about me. For one thing, I'm already a warrior of sorts. I happen to be a damn good gymnast." To punctuate what I'd said and to show him I could be spontaneous, I stood up from the couch and did a standing backward somersault, landing gracefully on the carpet.

"Hey," he said, "that's great. Do it again!"

"Oh, it's no big deal — pretty easy, actually." I smiled modestly. I was used to showing this sort of thing to kids at the beach or the park. They always wanted to see it again, too.

"All right now, Soc, watch closely." I leaped upward and was just turning over when someone or something tossed me through the air. I landed in a heap on the couch. The Mexican blanket from the back of the couch wrapped itself around me, covering me. I poked my head out from the covers quickly, looking for Socrates. He was still sitting across the room, twelve feet away, curled in his chair and smiling mischievously.

"How did you do that?" My confusion was as total as his look of innocence.

"Want to see it again?" he said. Then, seeing my expression, he added, "Don't feel badly about your little slip, Dan; even a great warrior like you can make a boo-boo now and then."

I stood numbly and straightened the couch, tucking the blanket back in. I had to do something with my hands; I needed time to think. How had he done it? Another question that would go unanswered.

Socrates padded softly out of the office to fill the tank of a pickup truck full of household belongings. Off to cheer up another traveler on his journey, I thought. Then I closed my eyes and pondered Soc's apparent defiance of natural laws, or at least, common sense.

"Would you like to learn some secrets?" I hadn't even heard him come in. He was seated in his chair, his legs crossed.

I crossed my legs, too, and leaned forward eagerly. Misjudging the softness of the couch, I leaned a little bit too far and tipped over. Before I could untangle my legs, I found myself sprawled facedown on the rug.

Socrates made an effort not to laugh. And failed. I sat up quickly, ramrod straight. One look at my stolid expression left Soc helpless with mirth. More accustomed to applause than ridicule, I leaped to my feet in shame and anger.

"Sit down!" Soc commanded, his voice charged with authority. He pointed to the couch. I sat. "I asked you if you wanted to hear a secret."

"I do — about rooftops."

"*You* get to choose whether or not you want to hear a secret. *I* choose what it is about."

"Why do we always have to play by your rules?"

"Because it's my station, that's why." Soc spoke with exaggerated petulance, possibly mocking me further. "Now pay close attention. By the way, are you comfortable and, uh, stable?" he winked.

I clenched my teeth but held my tongue.

"Dan, I have places to show you and tales to tell. I have secrets to unfold. But before we begin this journey together, you must appreciate that a secret's value is not in what you know, but in what you *do*."

Soc took an old dictionary from his drawer and held it in the air. "Use whatever knowledge you have but see its limitations. Knowledge alone does not suffice; it has no heart. No amount of knowledge will nourish or sustain your spirit; it can never bring you ultimate happiness or peace. Life requires more than knowledge; it requires intense feeling and constant energy. Life demands *right action* if knowledge is to come alive."

"I know that, Soc."

"That's your problem — you know but you don't *act*. You're no warrior."

"Socrates, I know at times I behave like a warrior, when the pressure is on — you should see me in the gym."

He nodded. "You may experience the mind of a warrior on occasion, resolute, flexible, clear, and free of doubt. You can develop the body of a warrior, lithe, supple, sensitive, and filled with energy. In rare moments, you may even feel the heart of a warrior, extending compassion to those around you. But these qualities are fragmented in you. You lack integration. My task is to put you back together again, Humpty."

"Wait a damn minute! I know you have some unusual talents and like to surround yourself with an air of mystery, but I don't see how you can presume to put *me* back together. Let's look at the situation: I'm a college student; you service cars. I'm a world champion; you tinker in the garage, make tea, and wait for some poor fool to walk in so you can frighten the wits out of him. Maybe I can help put *you* back together." I didn't quite know what I was saying, but it felt good.

Socrates laughed, shaking his head as if he couldn't believe what he'd just heard. Then he came over to me, knelt down at my side, looked into my eyes, and spoke softly. "Maybe you will have a chance someday. But for now, you should understand the difference between us." He poked me in the ribs, then poked me again and again, saying, "The warrior acts... "

"Damn it, stop that!" I yelled. "You're getting on my nerves!"

"...and the fool only reacts."

"Well, what do you expect?"

"I poke you and you get irritable; I insult you and you react with pride and anger; I slip on a banana peel and... " He took two steps away from me and slipped, landing with a thud on the rug. I couldn't hold it in. I bellowed.

He sat up on the floor and turned to face me, making a

final point. "Your feelings and reactions, Dan, are automatic and predictable; mine are not. I create my life spontaneously; yours is determined by your thoughts, your emotions, your past."

"How can you assume all this about me, about my past?"

"Because, I've been watching you for years."

"Sure you have," I said, waiting for the joke. None came.

It was getting late, and I had a lot to think about. I felt burdened by a new obligation, one I wasn't sure I could fulfill. Socrates came in, wiped his hands, and filled his mug with springwater. As he sipped slowly, I said, "I've got to go now, Soc. It's late and I have a lot of important schoolwork to do."

Socrates remained quietly seated as I stood and put on my jacket. Then, as I was about to go out the door, he spoke slowly and carefully. Each word had the effect of a gentle slap on my cheek.

"You had better reconsider your 'importances' if you are to have even a chance of becoming a warrior. Right now, you have the intelligence of a jackass; your spirit is mush. You do have a great deal of important work to do but in a different classroom than you now imagine."

I had been staring at the floor. I snapped my head up to face him, but I couldn't look him in the eye. I turned away.

"To survive the lessons ahead," he continued, "you're going to need far more energy than ever before. You'll have to cleanse your body of tension, free your mind of stagnant beliefs, and open your heart to loving-kindness."

"Soc, I'd better explain my time schedule. I want you to understand how busy I am. I'd like to visit with you often, but I have so little time."

He looked at me with somber eyes. "You have even less time than you might imagine."

"What do you mean?" I gasped.

"Never mind that now," he said. "Go on."

"Well, I have these goals. I want to be a champion gymnast.

I want my team to win the national championships. I want to graduate in good standing, and that means books to read and papers to write. What you seem to be offering me instead is staying up half the night in a gas station, listening to — I hope you won't take this as an insult — a very strange man who wants to draw me into his fantasy world. It's crazy!"

"Yes," he smiled sadly, "it is crazy." Socrates sat back in his chair and looked down at the floor. My mind rebelled at his helpless-old-man ploy, but my heart was drawn to this robust old eccentric who claimed to be some kind of warrior. I sat back down. Then a story that my grandfather had told me came to mind:

There was once a beloved king whose castle was on a high hill, overlooking his shire. He was so popular that the nearby townspeople sent him gifts daily, and his birthday celebration was enjoyed throughout the kingdom. The people loved him for his renowned wisdom and fair judgments.

One day, tragedy struck the town. The water supply was polluted, and every man, woman, and child went insane. Only the king, who had a private spring, was spared.

Soon after the tragedy, the mad townspeople began speaking of how the king was acting "strangely" and how his judgments were poor and his wisdom a sham. Many even went so far as to say that the king had gone crazy. His popularity soon vanished. No longer did the people bring him gifts or celebrate his birthday.

The lonely king, high on the hill, had no company at all. One day he decided to leave the hill and pay a visit to the town. It was a warm day, and so he drank from the village fountain.

That night there was a great celebration. The people rejoiced, for their beloved king had "regained his sanity."

I realized then that the crazy world that Socrates had referred to was not his world at all, but mine.

I stood, ready to leave. "Socrates, you've told me to listen to my own body intuition and not depend upon what I read or what people tell me. Why, then, should I sit quietly and listen to what you tell me?"

"A very good question," he answered. "There is an equally good answer. First of all, I speak to you from my own experience; I am not relating abstract theories I read in a book or heard secondhand from an expert. I am one who truly knows his own body and mind, and therefore knows others' as well. Besides," he smiled, "how do you know that I'm not your own intuition, speaking to you now?" He turned to his desk and picked up some paperwork. I had been dismissed for the evening. My whirling thoughts carried me into the night.

I was upset for days afterward. I felt weak and inadequate around this man, and I was angry about the way he treated me. He constantly seemed to underestimate me; I wasn't a child! Why should I choose to play a jackass sitting in a gas station, I thought, when here, in my domain, I'm admired and respected?

I trained harder than ever in gymnastics — my body burned as I flew and fought my way through routine after routine. Yet it was somehow less satisfying than before. Every time I learned a new move or received a compliment, I remembered being tossed through the air onto the couch by that old man.

Hal, my coach, became concerned about me and wanted to know if anything was wrong. I reassured him that everything was fine. But it wasn't. I didn't feel like joking around with the guys on the team anymore. I was just confused.

That night I dreamed of death again, but with a difference. A chortling Socrates, decked out in the Grim Reaper's gloomy getup, pointed a gun at me that went off, shooting out a flag that said, "Bang!" I woke up laughing for a change.

The next day I found a note in my mailbox. All it said was, "Rooftop secrets." When Socrates arrived at the station that night, I was already sitting on the steps, waiting for him.

23

I'd come early to question the day attendants about Socrates — to find out his real name, maybe even where he lived — but they didn't know anything about him. "Who cares anyway?" one yawned. "He's just some old geezer who likes the night shift."

Soc removed his windbreaker. "Well?" I pounced. "Are you finally going to tell me how you got up on the roof?"

"Yes, I am. I think you're ready to hear it," he said seriously.

"In ancient Japan, there existed an elite group of warrior assassins."

He said the last word with a hissing sound, making me acutely aware of the dark silence lurking outside. My neck started to get that prickly feeling again.

"These warriors," he continued, "were named *ninja*. The legends and reputation surrounding them were fearful. It was said that they could change themselves into animals; it was even said that they could fly — for short distances only, of course."

"Of course," I agreed, feeling the door to the dreamworld blow open with a chill gust. I wondered what he was leading up to, when he beckoned me into the garage, where he was working on a Japanese sports car.

"Got to change the plugs," Socrates said, ducking his head under the sleek hood.

"Yes, but what about the rooftop?" I urged.

"I'll get to it in a moment, as soon as I change these plugs. Be patient. What I'm about to tell you is worth waiting for, believe me."

I sat toying with a mallet lying on the worktable.

From Socrates' corner I heard, "You know, this is very amusing work, if you really pay attention to it." For him it was, perhaps.

Suddenly he put down the plugs, ran over to the light switch, and flicked it. In a darkness so total that I couldn't even see my hands in front of me, I began to get nervous. I never knew what Socrates would do, and after that talk about ninja. ...

"Soc? Soc?"

"Where are you?" he yelled from directly behind me.

I spun around and fell onto the hood of a Chevy. "I — I don't know!" I stammered.

"Absolutely right," he said, turning on the lights. "I guess you are getting smarter," he said, with a Cheshire cat grin.

I shook my head at his lunacy and perched myself on the Chevy's fender, glancing under the open hood to find its innards missing. "Socrates, will you quit clowning and get *on* with it?"

As he deftly screwed in the new plugs, unsnapped the distributor cap, and examined the rotors, he continued.

"These ninja were not practitioners of magic. Their secret was the most intense physical and mental training known to man."

"Socrates, where is all this leading?"

"To see where something leads, it's best to wait until you reach the end," he replied and continued with the story.

"The ninja could swim wearing heavy armor; they could climb sheer walls like lizards, using only fingers and toes in tiny cracks. They designed imaginative scaling ropes, dark and nearly invisible, and used clever means of hiding, tricks of distraction, illusion, and escape. The ninja," he finally added, "were great jumpers."

"Now we're getting somewhere!" I almost rubbed my hands in anticipation.

"The young warrior, when still a child, would be trained in jumping in the following manner: He was given a corn seed and told to plant it. Just as the stalk was beginning to grow, the young warrior would jump over the small stalk many, many times. Each day the stalk would grow; each day the child would jump. Soon the stalk was higher than the child's head, but that wouldn't stop him. Finally, if he failed to clear the stalk, he would be given a new seed and would begin over. Eventually, there was no stalk that the young ninja could not leap over."

"Well, then what? What is the secret?" I asked, waiting for the final revelation.

Socrates paused and took a deep breath. "So you see, the young ninja practiced with cornstalks. I practice with gas stations."

Silence filled the room. Then, suddenly, Soc's musical laughter pealed through the station; he was laughing so hard he had to lean against the Datsun he'd been working on.

"So that's it, huh? That's what you were going to tell me about rooftops?"

"Dan, that is all you can know until you can *do,*" he answered.

"You mean you're going to teach me how to jump up on the roof?" I asked, my demeanor suddenly brightening.

"Maybe, maybe not. For now, toss me that screwdriver, will you?"

I threw it to him. I swear he grabbed it out of the air while looking in the other direction! He finished with it quickly and tossed it back to me, yelling, "Heads up!" I dropped it and it fell to the floor with a loud clatter. This was exasperating; I didn't know how much more ridicule I could take.

The weeks passed quickly, and my sleepless nights became commonplace. Somehow, I adjusted. And there was another change: I found that my visits with Socrates were becoming even more interesting to me than gymnastics practice.

Each night while we serviced cars — he put the gas in, I did windows, and both of us joked with customers — he would encourage me to talk about my life. He was strangely silent about his own, meeting my questions with a terse "Later," or answering in complete non sequiturs.

When I asked him why he was so interested in the details of my life, he said, "I need to understand your personal illusions to grasp the scope of your illness. We are going to have to clear your mind before the door to the warrior's way can open."

"Don't you touch my mind. I like it just the way it is."

"If you really liked it the way it is, you wouldn't be here now. You've changed your mind many times in the past. Soon, you're going to do it in a more profound way." After that, I decided I was going to have to be very careful with this man. I didn't know him all that well, and I still wasn't sure how crazy he was.

As it was, Soc's style was constantly changing, unorthodox, humorous, and even bizarre. Once he ran screaming after a little white dog that had just peed on the station steps — right in the middle of a lecture he was giving me on the "supreme benefits of an unshakably serene composure."

Another time, about a week later, after we'd stayed up all night, we walked to Strawberry Creek and stood on a bridge, looking down at the stream overflowing with the winter rains.

"I wonder how deep the stream is today" I casually remarked, gazing absentmindedly down into the rushing waters. The next thing I knew, I'd splashed into the churning, muddy brown water.

He had tossed me off the bridge!

"Well, how deep is it?"

"Deep enough," I sputtered, dragging myself and my waterlogged clothes to shore. So much for idle speculation. I made a mental note to keep my mouth shut.

As the days passed I started to notice more and more differences between us. In the office, I'd devour candy bars when I got hungry; Soc munched on a fresh apple or pear or made himself herb tea. I fidgeted around on the couch while he sat serenely still on his chair, like a Buddha. My movements were awkward and noisy compared to the way he softly glided across the floor. And he was an old man, mind you.

27

There were many small lessons that awaited me each night, even in the early days. One night I made the mistake of complaining about how people at school just didn't seem to act very friendly toward me.

Softly, he said, "It is better for you to take responsibility for your life as it is, instead of blaming others, or circumstances, for your predicament. As your eyes open, you'll see that your state of health, happiness, and every circumstance of your life has been, in large part, arranged by you — consciously or unconsciously."

"I don't know what you mean, but I don't think I agree with it."

"I once knew a guy like you:

"I met him on a construction site in the Midwest. When the lunch whistle blew, all the workers would sit down together to eat. And every day, Sam would open his lunch pail and start to complain.

"'Son of a gun!' he'd cry, 'not peanut butter and jelly sandwiches again. I hate peanut butter and jelly!'

"He whined about his peanut butter and jelly sandwiches day after day after day until one of the guys on the work crew finally said, 'Fer crissakes, Sam, if you hate peanut butter and jelly so much, why don't you just tell yer ol' lady to make you something different?'

"'What do you mean, my ol' lady?' Sam replied. 'I'm not married. I make my own sandwiches.'"

Socrates paused, then added, "We all make our own sandwiches." He handed me a brown bag with two sandwiches in it. "Do you want the cheese and tomato or tomato and cheese?" he asked, grinning.

"Oh, just give me either," I jested back.

As we munched, Socrates said, "When you become fully responsible for your life, you can become fully human; once you become human, you may discover what it means to be a warrior."

"Thanks, Soc, for the food for thought, and for belly." I bowed grandly. Then I put on my jacket and got ready to leave. "I won't be by for a couple of weeks. Finals are coming up. And I also have some hard thinking to do." Before he could comment I waved good-bye and left for home.

I lost myself in the semester's last classes. My hours in the gym were spent in the hardest training I'd ever done. Whenever I stopped pushing myself, my thoughts and feelings began to stir uneasily. I felt the first signs of what was to become a growing sense of alienation from my everyday world. For the first time in my life, I had a choice between two distinct realities. One was crazy and one was sane — but I didn't know which was which, so I committed myself to neither.

I couldn't shake a growing sense that maybe, just maybe, Socrates was not so eccentric after all. Perhaps his descriptions of my life had been more accurate than I'd imagined. I began to really see how I acted with people, and what I saw began to disturb me. I was sociable enough on the outside, but I was really only concerned about myself.

Bill, one of my best friends, fell from the pommel horse and broke his wrist; Rick learned a full twisting back somersault that he'd been working on for a year. I felt the same emotional response in both cases: nothing.

Under the weight of my growing self-knowledge, my self-image was sinking fast.

One night, just before finals, I heard a knock at my door. I was surprised and happy to find toothpaste Susie, the blond cheerleader I hadn't seen in weeks. I realized how lonely I'd been.

"Aren't you going to invite me in, Danny?"

"Oh! Yes. I'm really glad to see you. Uh, sit down, let me take your coat. Would you like something to eat? Something to drink?" She just gazed at me.

"What is it, Susie?"

"You look tired, Danny, but..." she reached out and touched my face. "There's something...your eyes look different somehow. What is it?"

I touched her cheek. "Stay with me tonight, Susie."

"I thought you'd never ask. I brought my toothbrush."

The next morning I turned over to smell Sue's tousled hair, sweet like summer straw, and to feel her soft breath on my pillow. "I should feel good," I thought, but my mood was gray like the fog outside.

For the next few days, Sue and I spent a lot of time together. I don't think I was very good company, but Sue's spirits were enough for both of us.

Something kept me from telling her about Socrates. He was of another world, a world in which she had no part. How could she understand when I couldn't even fathom what was happening to me?

Finals came and went. I did well, but I didn't care. Susie went home for spring vacation, and I was glad to be alone.

Spring vacation was soon over, and warm winds blew through the littered streets of Berkeley. I knew that it was time to return to the warrior's world, to that strange little gas station — this time perhaps more open and more humble than before. But now I was more sure of one thing. If Socrates cut at me with his sharp wit again, I was going to slash right back.

BOOK ONE

THE WINDS OF CHANGE

CHAPTER ONE

GUSTS OF MAGIC

It was late evening. After my workout and dinner, I fell asleep. When I awoke it was nearly midnight. I walked slowly through the crisp night air of early spring toward the station. A strong breeze blew from behind me, as if impelling me forward along the campus paths.

As I neared the familiar intersection, I slowed down. A light drizzle had begun, chilling the night. In the glow from the warmly lit office I could see Soc's shape through the misted window, drinking from his mug, and a mixture of anticipation and dread squeezed my lungs and accelerated my heartbeat.

I looked down at the pavement as I crossed the street and neared the office door. The wind gusted against the back of my neck. Suddenly chilled, I snapped my head up to see Socrates standing in the doorway, staring at me and sniffing the air like a wolf. He seemed to be looking right through me. Memories of the Grim Reaper returned. I knew this man had within him great warmth and compassion, but I sensed that behind his dark eyes lay a great unknown danger.

My fear dissipated when he gently said, "It's good that you've returned." He welcomed me into the office with a wave of his arm. Just as I took off my shoes and sat down, the station bell clanged. I wiped the mist off the window and looked out to see an old Plymouth limp in with a flat tire. Socrates was already headed out the door wearing his army surplus rain poncho. Watching him, I wondered momentarily how he could possibly have frightened me.

Then rain clouds darkened the night, bringing back fleeting images of the black-hooded death of my dream, changing the pattering of the soft rain into bony fingers drumming madly on the roof. I moved restlessly on the couch, tired from my intense workouts in the gym. The conference championships were coming up next week, and today had been the last hard workout before the meet.

Socrates opened the door to the office. He stood with the door open and said, "Come outside — now," then left me. As I rose and put on my shoes, I looked through the mist. Socrates was standing out beyond the pumps, just outside the aura of the station lights. Half-shrouded in darkness, he appeared to be wearing a black hood.

The office now seemed like a fortress against the night — and against a world outside that was beginning to grate on my nerves like noisy downtown traffic. I was not going out there. Socrates beckoned me again, then again, from out in the darkness. Surrendering to fate, I went outside.

As I approached him cautiously, he said, "Listen, can you feel it?"

"What?"

"Feel!"

Just then the rain stopped and the wind seemed to change directions. Strange — a warm wind. "The wind, Soc?"

"Yes, the winds. They're changing. It means a turning point for you — now. You may not have realized it; neither did I, in fact — but tonight is a critical moment in time for you. You left, but you returned. And now the winds are changing." He looked at me for a moment, then strode back inside.

I followed him in and sat down on the familiar couch. Socrates was very still in his soft brown chair, his eyes riveted upon me. In a voice strong enough to pierce walls but light enough to be carried by the March winds, he announced, "There is something I must do now. Don't be afraid."

He stood. "Socrates, you're scaring the hell out of me!" I

stammered angrily, sliding back in the couch as he slowly came toward me, stalking, like a tiger on the prowl.

He glanced out the window for a moment, checking for possible interruptions, then knelt in front of me, saying softly, "Dan, do you recall that I told you we must work on changing your mind before you can see the warrior's way?"

"Yes, but I really don't think..."

"Don't be afraid," he repeated. "Comfort yourself with a saying of Confucius," he smiled. "'Only the supremely wise and the ignorant do not alter.'" Saying that, he reached out and placed his hands gently but firmly on my temples.

Nothing happened for a moment — then suddenly I felt a growing pressure in the middle of my head. There was a loud buzzing, then a sound like waves rushing up on the beach. I heard bells ringing, and my head felt as if it was going to burst. That's when I saw the light, and my mind exploded with its brightness. Something in me was dying — I knew this for a certainty — and something else was being born! Then the light engulfed everything.

I found myself lying back on the couch. Socrates was offering me a cup of tea, shaking me gently.

"What happened to me?"

"Let's just say I manipulated your energies and opened a few new circuits. The fireworks were just your brain's delight in the energy bath. The result is that you are relieved of your lifelong illusion of knowledge. From now on, ordinary knowledge is no longer going to satisfy you, I'm afraid."

"I don't get it."

"You will," he said, without smiling.

I was very tired. We sipped our tea in silence. Then, excusing myself, I rose, put on my sweater, and walked home as if in a dream.

The next day was full of classes and full of professors babbling words that had no meaning or relevance for me. In History 101, Watson lectured on how Churchill's political instincts had affected the war. I stopped taking notes. I was too busy taking in the colors and textures of the room, feeling the energies of the people around me. The sounds of my professors' voices were far more interesting than the concepts they conveyed. Socrates, what did you do to me? I'll never make it through finals.

I was walking out of class, fascinated by the knobby texture of the carpet, when I heard a familiar voice.

"Hi, Danny! I haven't seen you for days. I've called every night, but you're never home. Where have you been hiding?"

"Oh, hi Susie. It's good to see you again. I've been... studying." Her words had danced through the air. I could hardly understand them, but I could feel what she was feeling — hurt and a little jealous. Yet her face was beaming as usual.

"I'd like to talk more, Susie, but I'm on my way to the gym."

"Oh, I forgot." I felt her disappointment. "Well," she said, "I'll see you soon, huh?"

"Sure."

"Hey," she said. "Wasn't Watson's lecture great? I just love hearing about Churchill's life. Isn't it interesting?"

"Uh, yeah — great lecture."

"Well, bye for now, Danny."

"Bye." Turning away, I recalled what Soc had said about my "shyness and fear." Maybe he was right. I wasn't really that comfortable with people; I was never sure of what to say. But in the gym that afternoon, I knew exactly what to *do*. I came alive, turning on the faucet of my energy full blast. I played, swung, leaped; I was a clown, a magician, a chimpanzee. It was one of my best days ever. My mind was so clear that I felt exactly how to do anything I tried. My body was relaxed, supple, quick, and light. In tumbling, I invented a one and one-half backward somersault with a late half twist to a roll; from the high bar, I swung into a full twisting double flyaway — both moves the first ever done in the United States.

A few days later, the team flew up to Oregon for the conference championships. We won the meet and returned home to fanfare and glory — but I couldn't escape the concerns that plagued me.

I considered the events that had occurred since the other night's experience of the bursting light. Something had certainly happened, as Soc had predicted, but it was frightening and I didn't think I liked it at all. Perhaps Socrates was not what he seemed; perhaps he was something more clever, or more evil than I'd suspected.

These thoughts vanished as I stepped through the doorway of the lighted office and saw his eager smile. As soon as I'd sat down, Socrates said, "Are you ready to go on a journey?"

"A journey?" I echoed.

"Yes — a trip, travel, sojourn, vacation — an adventure."

"No, thanks, I'm not dressed for it."

"Nonsense!" he bellowed, so loudly that we both looked around to see if any passersby had heard. "Shhh!" he whispered loudly. "Not so loud, you'll wake everyone."

Taking advantage of his affability, I blurted out, "Socrates, my life no longer makes sense. Nothing works, except when I'm in the gym. Aren't you supposed to make things better for me? I thought that's what a teacher did."

He started to speak, but I interrupted.

"And another thing. I've always believed that we have to find our own paths in life. No one can tell another how to live."

Socrates slapped his forehead with his palm, then looked upward in resignation. "I am part of your path, baboon. And I didn't exactly rob you from the cradle and lock you up here, you know. You can take off whenever you like." He walked to the door and held it open.

Just then, a black limousine pulled into the station, and Soc affected a British accent: "Your car is ready, sir." Disoriented, I actually thought we were going on a trip in the limousine. I mean, why not? So, befuddled, I walked straight out to the limo and started to climb into the backseat. I found myself staring into the wrinkled old face of a little man, sitting with his arm around a girl of about sixteen, probably off the streets of Berkeley. He stared at me like a hostile lizard.

Soc's hand grabbed me by the back of my sweater and dragged me out of the car. Closing the door, he apologized: "Excuse my young friend. He's never been in a beautiful car like this and just got carried away — didn't you, Jack?"

I nodded dumbly. "What's going on?" I whispered fiercely out of the side of my mouth. But he was already washing the

windows. When the car pulled away, I flushed with embar-
rassment. "Why didn't you stop me, Socrates?"

"Frankly, it was pretty funny. I hadn't realized you could
be so gullible."

We stood there, in the middle of the night, staring each
other down. Socrates grinned as I clenched my teeth. I was getting angry. "I'm really tired of playing the fool around you!" I
yelled.

"But you've been practicing so diligently, you've got it
nearly perfect."

I wheeled around, kicked the trash can, and stomped back
toward the office. I called back to him, "Why did you call me
Jack, a while ago?"

"Short for jackass," he said.

"All right, goddamn it," I said as I ran by him to enter the
office. "Let's go on your journey. Whatever you want to give, I
can take. Now where are we headed? Where am I headed?"

Socrates took a deep breath. "Dan, I can't tell you this —
at least not in so many words. Much of a warrior's path is
subtle, invisible to the uninitiated. For now, I have been
showing you what a warrior is *not* by showing you your own
mind. You can come to understand that soon enough."

Now he led me to a cubbyhole I hadn't noticed before,
hidden behind the racks of tools in the garage and furnished
with a small rug and a heavy straight-backed chair. The pre-
dominant color of the nook was gray. My stomach felt
queasy.

"Sit down," he said gently.

"Not until you explain what this is all about." I crossed my
arms over my chest.

Socrates sighed. "*I* am a warrior; *you* are a baboon. Now
choose: you can sit down and shut up — or you can go back
to your gymnastics spotlight and forget you ever knew me."

"You're serious?"

"Yes, I am."

I hesitated a second, then sat.

Socrates reached into a drawer, took out some long pieces
of cotton cloth, and began to tie me to the chair.

"What are you going to do, torture me?" I half-joked.

"No. Now please be silent," he said, tying the last strip around my waist and behind the chair, like an airline seatbelt.

"Are we going flying, Soc?" I asked nervously.

"In a manner of speaking, yes," he said, kneeling in front of me, taking my head in his hands and placing his thumbs against the upper ridges of my eye sockets. My teeth chattered; I had an excruciating urge to urinate. But in another second, I had forgotten all. Colored lights flashed. I thought I heard his voice but couldn't quite make it out; it was too far away.

We were walking down a corridor swathed in a blue fog. My feet moved but I couldn't feel ground. Gigantic trees surrounded us; they became buildings; the buildings became boulders, and we ascended a steep canyon that became the edge of a sheer cliff.

The fog had cleared; the air was freezing. Green clouds stretched below us for miles, meeting an orange sky on the horizon.

I was shaking. I tried to say something to Socrates, but my voice came out muffled. My shaking grew uncontrollable. Soc put his hand on my belly. It was very warm and had a wondrously calming effect. I relaxed and he took my arm firmly, tightening his grip, and hurtled forward, off the edge of the world, pulling me with him.

Without warning the clouds disappeared and we were hanging from the rafters of an indoor stadium, swinging precariously like two drunken spiders high above the floor.

"Ooops," said Soc. "Slight miscalculation."

"What the hell!" I yelled, struggling for a better handhold. I swung myself up and over and lay panting on a beam, twining my arms and legs around it. Socrates had already perched himself lightly on the beam in front of me. I noticed that he handled himself well for an old man.

"Hey, look," I pointed. "It's a gymnastics meet! Socrates, you're nuts."

"*I'm* nuts?" he laughed quietly. "Look who's sitting on the beam next to me."

"How are we going to get down?"

"Same way we got up, of course."

"How *did* we get up here?"

He scratched his head. "I'm not precisely sure; I had hoped for a front-row seat. I guess they were sold out."

I began to laugh shrilly. This whole thing was too ridiculous. Soc clapped a hand over my mouth. "Shhhh!" He removed his hand. That was a mistake.

"HaHaHaHaHa!" I laughed loudly before he muffled me again. I calmed down but felt giddy and started giggling.

He whispered at me harshly. "This journey is real — more real than the waking dreams of your usual life. Pay attention!"

By this time the scene below had indeed caught my attention. The audience, from this height, coalesced into a multicolored array of dots, a shimmering, rippling, pointillist painting. I caught sight of a raised platform in the middle of the arena with a familiar bright blue square of floor exercise mat, surrounded by various gymnastics apparatus. My stomach rumbled in response; I experienced my usual precompetition nervousness.

Socrates reached into a small knapsack (where had that come from?) and handed me binoculars, just as a female performer walked out onto the floor.

I focused my binoculars on the lone gymnast and saw she was from the Soviet Union. So, we were attending an international exhibition somewhere. As she walked over to the uneven bars, I realized that I could hear her talking to herself! "The acoustics in here," I thought, "must be fantastic." But then I saw that her lips weren't moving.

I moved the lenses quickly to the audience and heard the roar of many voices; yet they were just sitting quietly. Then it came to me. Somehow, I was reading their minds!

I turned the glasses back to the woman gymnast. In spite of the language barrier, I could understand her thoughts: "Be strong...ready...." I saw a preview of her routine as she ran through it mentally.

Then I focused on a man in the audience, a guy in a white sport shirt in the midst of a sexual fantasy about one of the East German contestants. Another man, apparently a coach, was engrossed with the woman about to perform. A woman in the audience watched her, too, thinking, "Beautiful girl... had a bad fall last year... hope she does a good job."

I noticed that I was not receiving words, but feeling-concepts — sometimes quiet or muffled, sometimes loud and clear. That was how I could "understand" Russian, German, or whatever.

I noticed something else. When the Soviet gymnast was doing her routine, her mind was quiet. When she finished and returned to her chair, her mind started up again. It was the same for the East German gymnast on the rings and the American on the horizontal bar. Furthermore, the best performers had the quietest minds during their moment of truth.

One East German fellow was distracted by a noise while he swung through handstand after handstand on the parallel bars. I sensed his mind drawn to the noise; he thought, "What?..." as he muffed his final somersault to handstand.

A telepathic voyeur, I peeked into the minds of the audience. "I'm hungry....Got to catch an eleven o'clock plane or the Dusseldorf plans are shot....I'm hungry!" But as soon as a performer was in midflight, the minds of the audience calmed, too.

For the first time, I realized why I loved gymnastics so. It gave me a blessed respite from my noisy mind. When I was swinging and somersaulting, nothing else mattered. When my body was active, my mind rested in the moments of silence.

The mental noise from the audience was getting annoying, like a stereo playing too loud. I lowered my glasses and let them hang. But I had neglected to fasten the strap around my neck, and I almost fell off the rafter trying to grab them as they plummeted straight for the floor exercise mat and a woman performer directly below!

"Soc!" I whispered in alarm. He sat placidly. I looked down to see the damage, but the binoculars had disappeared.

Socrates grinned. "Things work under a slightly different set of laws when you travel with me."

He disappeared and I was tumbling through space, not downward but upward. I had a vague sense of walking backward from the edge of a cliff, down a canyon, then into a mist, like a character in a crazy movie in reverse.

Socrates was wiping my face with a wet cloth. Still strapped to the chair, I slumped.

"Well," he said. "Isn't travel broadening?"

"You can say that again. Uh, how about unstrapping me?"

"Not just yet," he replied, reaching again for my head.

I mouthed, "No, wait!" just before the lights went out and a howling wind arose, carrying me off into space and time.

I became the wind, yet with eyes and ears. And I saw and heard far and wide. I blew past the east coast of India near the Bay of Bengal, past a scrubwoman busy with her tasks. In Hong Kong, I whirled around a seller of fine fabric bargaining loudly with a shopper. I raced through the streets of São Paulo, drying the sweat of German tourists playing volleyball in the hot tropical sun.

I left no country untouched. I thundered through China and Mongolia and across the vast, rich land of the Soviet Union. I gusted through the valleys and alpine meadows of Austria, sliced cold through the fjords of Norway. I tossed up litter on the Rue Pigalle in Paris. One moment I was a twister, ripping across Texas; the next I was a gentle breeze, caressing the hair of a young girl contemplating suicide in Canton, Ohio.

I experienced every emotion, heard every cry of anguish and every peal of laughter. Every human circumstance was opened to me. I felt it all, and I understood.

The world was peopled with minds, whirling faster than any wind, in search of distraction and escape from the predicament of change, the dilemma of life and death — seeking purpose, security, enjoyment, trying to make sense of the mystery. Everyone everywhere lived a confused, bitter search. Reality never matched their dreams; happiness was just around the corner — a corner they never turned.

And the source of it all was the human mind.

Socrates was removing the cloth strips that had bound me. Sunlight streaked through the windows of the garage into my eyes — eyes that had seen so much — filling them with tears.

Socrates helped me into the office. As I lay trembling on the couch, I realized that I was no longer the naive and self-important youth who had sat quaking in the gray chair a few minutes or hours or days ago. I felt very old. I had seen the suffering of the world, the condition of the human mind, and I almost wept with an inconsolable sadness. There was no escape.

Socrates, on the other hand, was jovial. "Well, no more time to play games right now. My shift is almost up. Why don't you shuffle on home and get some sleep, kiddo."

I creaked to my feet and put my arm in the wrong sleeve of my jacket. Extricating myself, I asked weakly, "Socrates, why'd you tie me down?"

"Never too weak for questions, I see. I tied you down so you wouldn't fall off the chair while you were thrashing around playing Peter Pan."

"Did I really fly? I felt like it." I sat down again, heavily.

"Let's say for now that it was a flight of the imagination."

"Did you hypnotize me or what?"

"Not in the way you mean — certainly not to the same degree you've been hypnotized by your own confused mental processes." He laughed, picked up his knapsack (where had I seen it before?), and prepared to leave. "What I did was draw you into one of many parallel realities — for your amusement and instruction."

"How?"

"It's a bit complicated. Why don't we leave it for another time." Socrates yawned and stretched like a cat. As I stumbled out the door I heard Soc's voice behind me. "Sleep well. You can expect a little surprise when you awake."

"Please, no more surprises," I mumbled, heading for home in a daze. I vaguely remember falling onto my bed. Then blackness.

I awoke to the sound of the windup clock ticking loudly on the blue chest of drawers. But I owned no windup clock; I had no blue chest of drawers. Neither did I possess this thick quilt now in disarray at my feet. Then I noticed that the feet weren't mine either. Much too small, I thought. The sun poured through the unfamiliar picture window.

Who and where was I? I held on to a quickly fading memory, then it was gone.

My small feet kicked off the remaining covers, and I leaped out of bed, just as Mom yelled, "Danneeeey — time to get up, sweetheart." It was February 22, 1952 — my sixth birthday. I let my pajamas fall to the floor and kicked them under the bed, then ran downstairs in my Lone Ranger underwear. In a few hours my friends would be arriving with presents, and we'd have cake and ice cream and lots of fun!

After all the party decorations were thrown out and everyone had gone, I played listlessly with my new toys. I was bored, I was tired, and my stomach hurt. I closed my eyes and floated off to sleep.

I saw each day pass like the next; school for a week, then the weekend, school, weekend, summer, fall, winter, and spring.

The years passed, and before long, I was one of the top high school gymnasts in Los Angeles. In the gym, life was exciting; outside the gym, it was a general disappointment. My few moments of fun consisted of bouncing on the trampoline or cuddling in the backseat of my Valiant with Phyllis, my first curvy girlfriend.

One day coach Harold Frey called me from Berkeley, California, and offered me a scholarship to the university. I couldn't wait to head up the coast to a new life. Phyllis, however, didn't share my enthusiasm. We began arguing about my going away, and we finally broke up. I felt bad but was consoled by my college plans. Soon, I was sure, life was really going to begin.

The college years raced by, filled with gymnastics victories but very few other high points. In my senior year, just before the Olympic gymnastics trials, I married Susie. We stayed in Berkeley so I could train with the team; I was so busy I didn't have much time or energy for my new wife.

The final trials were held at UCLA. When the scores were tallied, I was ecstatic — I'd made the team! But my performances at the Olympiad didn't live up to my expectations. I returned home and slipped into relative anonymity.

My newborn son arrived, and I began to feel a growing responsibility and pressure. I found a job selling life insurance, which took up most of my days and nights. I never seemed to have time for my family. Within a year Susie and I were separated; eventually she filed for divorce. A fresh start, I reflected sadly.

One day I looked in the mirror and realized that forty years had passed; I was old. Where had my life gone? With the help of my psychiatrist I had overcome my drinking problem; and I'd had money, houses, and women. But I had no one now. I was lonely.

I lay in bed late at night and wondered where my son was — it had been years since I'd seen him. I wondered about Susie and about my friends from the good old days.

I now passed the days in my favorite rocking chair, sipping wine, watching TV, and thinking about old times. I watched children play in front of the house. It had been a good life, I supposed. I'd gotten everything I'd gone after, so why wasn't I happy?

One day, one of the children playing on the lawn came up to the porch. A friendly little boy, smiling, he asked me how old I was.

"I'm two hundred years old," I said.

He giggled, said, "No you're not," and put his hands on his hips. I laughed, too, which touched off one of my coughing spells, and Mary, my pretty, capable young nurse, had to ask him to go.

After she had helped me regain my breath, I gasped, "Mary, will you let me be alone for a while?"

"Of course, Mr. Millman." I didn't watch her walk away — that was one of life's pleasures that had died long ago.

I sat alone. I had been alone my whole life, it seemed. I lay back on my rocker and breathed. My last pleasure. And soon that, too, would be gone. I cried soundlessly and bitterly. "Goddamn it!" I thought. "Why did my marriage have to fail? How could I have done things differently? How could I really have lived?"

Suddenly I felt a terrible, nagging fear, the worst of my life. Was it possible that I had missed something very important — something that would have made a real difference? No, impossible, I assured myself. I cited all my achievements aloud. The fear persisted.

I stood up slowly, looked down at the town from the porch of my hilltop house, and wondered: Where had life gone? What was it for? Was everyone… "Oh, my heart, it's — ahh, my arm, the pain!" I tried to call out, but couldn't breathe.

My knuckles grew white as I clutched the railing, trembling. Then my body turned to ice, and my heart to stone. I fell back into the chair; my head dropped forward.

The pain left abruptly, and there were lights I'd never seen before and sounds I'd never heard. Visions floated by.

"Is that you, Susie?" said a distant voice in my mind. Finally, all sight and sound became a point of light, then vanished.

I had found the only peace I'd ever known.

I heard a warrior's laugh. I sat up with a shock, the years pouring back into me. I was in my own bed, in my apartment, in Berkeley, California. I was still in college, and my clock showed 6:25 P.M. I'd slept through classes and workout!

I leaped out of bed and looked in the mirror, touching my still-youthful face, shivering with relief. It had all been a dream — a lifetime in a single dream, Soc's "little surprise."

I sat in my apartment and stared out the window, troubled. My dream had been exceptionally vivid. In fact, the past had been entirely accurate, even down to details I'd long forgotten. Socrates had told me that these journeys were real. Had this one predicted my future, too?

I hurried to the station and met Socrates as he arrived. As soon as he stepped inside and the day-shift attendant left, I asked, "All right, Soc. What happened?"

"You know better than I. It was your life, not mine, thank God."

"Socrates, I'm pleading with you" — I held out my hands

to him. "Is that what my life is going to be like? Because if it is, I see no point in living it."

He spoke very slowly and softly, as he did when he had something he wanted me to pay particular attention to. "Just as there are different interpretations of the past and many ways to change the present, there are any number of possible futures. What you dreamed was a highly probable future — the one you were headed for had you not met me."

"You mean that if I had decided to pass by the gas station that night, that dream would have been my future?"

"Very possibly. And it still may be. But you can make choices and change your present circumstances. You can alter your future."

Socrates made us some tea and set my mug down softly next to me. His movements were graceful, deliberate.

"Soc," I said, "I don't know what to make of it. My life these past months has been like an improbable novel, you know what I mean? Sometimes I wish I could go back to a normal life. This secret life here with you, these dreams and journeys — it's been hard on me."

Socrates took a deep breath; something of great import was coming. "Dan, I'm going to increase my demands on you as you become ready. I guarantee that you'll want to leave the life you know and choose alternatives that seem more attractive, more pleasant, more 'normal.' Right now, however, that would be a greater mistake than you can imagine."

"But I *do* see the value in what you're showing me."

"That may be so, but you still have an astonishing capacity to fool yourself. That is why you needed to dream your life. Remember it when you're tempted to run off and pursue your illusions."

"Don't worry about me, Socrates. I can handle it."

If I had known what was ahead, I would have kept my mouth shut.

CHAPTER TWO

THE WEB OF ILLUSION

The March winds were calming. Colorful spring blossoms spread their fragrance through the air — even into the shower room, where I washed the sweat and soreness from my body after an energy-filled workout.

I dressed quickly and skipped down the rear steps of Harmon Gym to watch the sky over Edwards Field turn orange with the sun's final glow. The cool air refreshed me. Relaxed and at peace with the world, I ambled downtown to get a cheeseburger on the way to the U.C. Theater. Tonight they were showing *The Great Escape,* about a daring escape of British and American prisoners of war.

When the film was over I jogged up University Avenue toward campus, heading left up Shattuck, and arrived at the station soon after Socrates came on duty. It was a busy night, so I helped him until just after midnight. We went into the office and washed our hands, after which he surprised me by starting to fix a Chinese dinner — and beginning a new phase in his teaching.

It started when I told him about the movie.

"Sounds like an exciting film," he said, unpacking the bag of fresh vegetables he'd brought in, "and an appropriate one, too."

"Oh? How's that?"

"You, too, Dan, need to escape. You're a prisoner of your own illusions — about yourself and about the world. To cut yourself free, you're going to need more courage and strength than any movie hero."

I felt so good that night I just couldn't take Soc seriously at all. "I don't feel like I'm in prison — except when you have me strapped to a chair."

He began washing vegetables. Over the sound of running water, he commented, "You don't see your prison because its bars are invisible. Part of my task is to point out your predicament, and I hope it is the most disillusioning experience of your life."

"Well thanks a lot, friend," I said, surprised by his ill wishes.

"I don't think you understand." He pointed a turnip at me, then sliced it into a bowl. "Disillusion is the greatest gift I can give you. But, because of your fondness for illusion, you consider the term negative. You commiserate with a friend by saying, 'Oh, what a disillusioning experience that must have been,' when you ought to be celebrating with him. The word *dis-illusion* is literally a 'freeing from illusion.' But you cling to your illusions."

"Facts," I challenged him.

"Facts," he said, tossing aside the tofu he'd been dicing. "Dan, you are suffering; you do not fundamentally enjoy your life. Your entertainments, your playful affairs, and even your gymnastics are temporary ways to distract you from your underlying sense of fear."

"Wait a minute, Soc." I was irritated. "Are you saying that gymnastics and sex and movies are bad?"

"Of course not. But for you they're addictions, not enjoyments. You use them to distract you from your chaotic inner life — the parade of regrets, anxieties, and fantasies you call your mind."

"Wait, Socrates. Those aren't facts."

"Yes, they are, and they are entirely verifiable, even though you don't see it yet. In your habitual quest for achievement and entertainment, you avoid the fundamental source of your suffering." He paused. "That was not something you really wanted to hear, was it?"

"Not particularly. And I don't think it applies to me. You have anything a little more upbeat?" I asked.

"Sure," he said, picking up his vegetables and resuming his chopping. "The truth is that life is going wonderfully for you and that you're not really suffering at all. You don't need me and you're already a warrior. How does that sound?"

"Better!" I laughed. But I knew it wasn't true. "The truth probably lies somewhere in between, don't you think?"

Without taking his eyes off the vegetables, Socrates said, "Your 'in between' is hell, from my perspective."

Defensively I asked, "Is it just me who's the moron, or do you specialize in working with the spiritually handicapped?"

"You might say that," he smiled, pouring sesame oil into a wok and setting it on the hot plate to warm. "But nearly all of humanity shares your predicament."

"And what predicament is that?"

"I thought I had already explained that," he said patiently. "If you don't get what you want, you suffer; if you get what you don't want, you suffer; even when you get exactly what you want, you still suffer because you can't hold on to it forever. Your *mind* is your predicament. It wants to be free of change, free of pain, free of the obligations of life and death. But change is a law, and no amount of pretending will alter that reality."

"Socrates, you can really be depressing, you know that? I don't even think I'm hungry anymore. If life is nothing but suffering, then why bother at all?"

"Life is not suffering; it's just that you will suffer it, rather than enjoy it, until you let go of your mind's attachments and just go for the ride freely, no matter what happens."

Socrates dropped the vegetables and tofu into the sizzling wok, stirring. A delicious aroma filled the office as he divided the crisp vegetables onto two plates and set them on his old desk, which served as our dining table.

"I think I just got my appetite back," I said.

Socrates laughed, then ate in silence, taking small morsels

with his chopsticks. I gobbled the food in about thirty seconds; I guess I really was hungry. While Socrates finished his meal, I asked him, "So what are the positive uses of the mind?"

He looked up from his plate. "There aren't any." With that, he calmly returned to his meal.

"Aren't any! Socrates, that's really crazy. What about the creations of the mind? The books, libraries, arts? What about all the advances of our society that were generated by brilliant minds?"

He grinned, put down his chopsticks, and said, "There aren't any brilliant minds." Then he carried the plates to the sink.

"Socrates, stop making these irresponsible statements and explain yourself!"

He emerged from the bathroom, bearing aloft two shining plates. "I'd better redefine some terms for you. 'Mind' is one of those slippery terms like 'love.' The proper definition depends on your state of consciousness. Look at it this way: You have a brain that directs the body, stores information, and plays with that information. We refer to the brain's abstract processes as 'the intellect.' Nowhere have I mentioned mind. The brain and the mind are not the same. The brain is real; the mind isn't.

"'Mind' is an illusory reflection of cerebral fidgeting. It comprises all the random, uncontrolled thoughts that bubble into awareness from the subconscious. Consciousness is not mind; awareness is not mind; attention is not mind. Mind is an obstruction, an aggravation. It is a kind of evolutionary mistake in the human being, a primal weakness in the human experiment. I have no use for the mind."

I sat in silence, breathing slowly. I didn't exactly know what to say. Soon enough, though, the words came. "I'm not sure what you're talking about, but you sound really sincere."

He just smiled and shrugged.

"Soc," I continued, "do I cut off my head to get rid of my mind?"

Smiling, he said, "That's one cure, but it has undesirable side effects. The brain can be a tool. It can recall phone numbers, solve math puzzles, or create poetry. In this way, it works for the rest of the body, like a tractor. But when you can't stop thinking of that math problem or phone number, or when troubling thoughts and memories arise without your intent, it's not your brain working, but your mind wandering. Then the mind controls you; then the tractor has run wild."

"I get it."

"To really get it, you must observe yourself to see what I mean. You have an angry thought bubble up and you *become* angry. It is the same with all your emotions. They're your knee-jerk responses to thoughts you can't control. Your thoughts are like wild monkeys stung by a scorpion."

"Socrates, I think..."

"You think too much!"

"I was just going to tell you that I'm really willing to change. That's one thing about me; I've always been open to change."

"That," said Socrates, "is one of your biggest illusions. You've been willing to change clothes, hairstyles, women, apartments, and jobs. You are all too willing to change anything except yourself, but change you will. Either I help you open your eyes or time will, but time is not always gentle," he said ominously. "Take your choice. But first realize that you're in prison — then we can plot your escape."

With that, he pulled up to his desk, picked up a pencil, and began checking off receipts, looking like a busy executive. I got the distinct feeling I'd been dismissed for the evening. I was glad class was out.

For the next couple of days, which soon stretched to weeks, I was too busy, I told myself, to drop in and visit with Socrates. But his words rattled around in my mind; I became preoccupied with its contents.

I started keeping a small notebook in which I wrote down my thoughts during the day — except for workouts, when my thoughts gave way to action. In two days I had to buy a bigger notebook; in a week, that was full. I was astounded to see the bulk and general negativity of my thought processes.

This practice increased my awareness of my mental noise; I'd turned up the volume on my thoughts that had only been subconscious background Muzak before. I stopped writing, but still the thoughts blared. Maybe Soc could help me with the volume control. I decided to visit him that night.

I found him in the garage, steam-cleaning the engine of an old Chevrolet. I was just about to speak when the small, dark-haired figure of a young woman appeared in the doorway. Not even Soc had heard her enter, which was very unusual. He saw her just before I did and glided toward her with open arms. She danced toward him and they hugged, whirling around the room. For the next few minutes, they just looked into each other's eyes. Socrates would ask, "Yes?" and she'd answer, "Yes." It was pretty bizarre.

With nothing else to do, I stared at her each time she whirled by. She was a little over five feet tall, sturdy looking, yet with an aura of delicate fragility. Her long black hair was tied in a bun, pulled back from a clear, shining complexion. The most notice-able feature on her face was her eyes — large, dark eyes.

My gaping must have finally caught their attention.

Socrates said, "Dan, this is Joy."

"Is Joy your name or a description of your mood?" I asked, trying to be clever.

"Both," she replied, " — most of the time." She looked at Socrates; he nodded. Then, to my surprise, she embraced me. Her arms wrapped softly around my waist in a very tender hug. I felt a rush of energy race up my spine. And I was instantly love-struck.

Joy looked at me with large, luminous eyes above a sweet, mischievous smile, and my own eyes glazed over. "The old Buddha's been putting you through the wringer, has he?" she said softly.

"Uh, I guess so," I muttered.

"Well, the squeeze is worth it. I know, he got to me first."

My mouth was too weak to ask for the details. Besides, she turned to Socrates and said, "I'm going now. Why don't we all meet here Saturday morning at ten and go up to Tilden Park for a picnic? I'll make lunch. It looks like good weather. OK?" She looked at Soc, then at me. I nodded dumbly as she sound-lessly floated out the door.

I was no help to Socrates for the rest of the evening. In fact, the rest of the week was a total loss. Finally, when Saturday came, I walked shirtless to the bus station. I was looking forward to getting some spring tan, and also hoped to impress Joy with my muscular torso.

We took the bus up to the park and walked cross-country over crackling leaves scattered in thick piles among the pine, birch, and elm trees surrounding us. We unpacked the food on a grassy knoll in full view of the warm sun. I flopped down on the blanket, anxious to roast in the sun, and hoped Joy would join me.

Without warning, the wind picked up and clouds gathered. I couldn't believe it. It had begun to rain — first a drizzle, then a sudden downpour. I grabbed my shirt and put it on, cursing. Socrates only laughed.

"How can you think this is funny!" I chided him. "We're getting soaked, there's no bus for an hour, and the food's ruined. Joy made the food; I'm sure she doesn't think it's so..." Joy was laughing, too.

"I'm not laughing at the rain," Soc said. "I'm laughing at *you*." He roared, and rolled in the wet leaves. Joy started doing a dance routine to "Singin' in the Rain." Debbie Reynolds and the Buddha — it was too much.

The rain ended as suddenly as it had begun. The sun broke through and soon our food and clothes were dry.

"I guess my rain dance worked." Joy took a bow.

As Joy sat behind my slumped form and gave my shoulders a rub, Socrates spoke. "It's time you began learning from your life experiences instead of complaining about them, or basking in them, Dan. Two very important lessons just offered themselves to you; they fell out of the sky, so to speak." I dug into the food, trying not to listen.

"First," he said, munching on some lettuce, "neither your disappointment nor your anger was caused by the rain."

My mouth was too full of potato salad for me to protest. Socrates continued, regally waving a carrot slice at me.

"The rain was a perfectly lawful display of nature. Your 'upset' at the ruined picnic and your 'happiness' when the sun reappeared were the product of your thoughts. They had nothing to do with the actual events. Haven't you been 'unhappy' at celebrations for example? It is obvious then that your mind, not other people or your surroundings, is the source of your moods. That is the first lesson."

Swallowing his potato salad, Soc said, "The second lesson comes from observing how you became even more angry when you noticed that I wasn't upset in the least. You began to see yourself compared to a warrior — two warriors, if you please." He grinned at Joy. "You didn't like that, did you, Dan? It might have implied a change was necessary."

I sat morosely, absorbing what he'd said. I was hardly aware that he and Joy had darted off. Soon it was drizzling again.

Socrates and Joy came back to the blanket. Socrates started jumping up and down, mimicking my earlier behavior. "Damn rain!" he yelled. "There goes our picnic!" He stomped back and forth, then stopped in mid-stomp and winked at me, grinning mischievously. Then he dove onto his belly in a puddle of wet leaves and pretended to be swimming. Joy started singing, or laughing — I couldn't tell which.

I just let go then and started rolling around with them in the wet leaves, wrestling with Joy. I particularly enjoyed that part, and I think she did, too. We ran and danced wildly until it was time to leave. Joy romped like a playful puppy, yet with all the qualities of a woman warrior. I was sinking fast.

As the bus rocked and rolled its way down the curving hills overlooking the bay, the sky turned pink and gold in the sunset. Socrates made a feeble attempt to summarize my lessons while I did my best to ignore him and snuggle with Joy in the backseat.

"Ahem — if I may have your attention," he said. He reached over, took my nose between two of his fingers, and turned my face toward him.

"Wad to you wad?" I asked. Joy was whispering in my ear as Socrates held on to my nose. "I'd rather listed to her thad to you," I said.

"She'll only lead you down the primrose path," he grinned,

releasing my nose. "Even a young fool in the throes of lust cannot fail to see how his mind creates both his disappointments and his — joys."

"An excellent choice of words," I said, losing myself in Joy's eyes.

As the bus rounded the bend we all sat quietly, watching San Francisco turn on her lights. The bus stopped at the bottom of the hill. Joy rose quickly and got off the bus, followed by Socrates. I started to follow, but he glanced back and said, "No." That was all. Joy looked at me through the open window.

"Joy, when will I see you again?"

"Perhaps soon. It depends," she said.

"Depends on what?" I said. "Joy, wait, don't go. Driver, let me off!" But the bus was pulling away from them. Joy and Soc had already disappeared into the darkness.

Sunday I sank into a deep depression over which I had no control. Monday in class I hardly heard a word my professor said. I was preoccupied during the workout, and my energy was drained. I'd not eaten since the picnic. I prepared myself for my Monday-night gas station visit. If I found Joy there I'd make her leave with me — or I'd leave with her.

She was there, all right, laughing with Socrates when I entered the office. Feeling like a stranger, I wondered if they were laughing at me. I went in, took off my shoes, and sat.

"Well, Dan, are you any smarter than you were on Saturday?" Socrates said. Joy smiled, and her smile hurt. Socrates added, "I wasn't sure you'd show up tonight, for fear I might say something you didn't want to hear." His words were like small hammers. I clenched my teeth.

"Try to relax, Dan," Joy said. I knew she was trying to help, but I felt overwhelmed, criticized by both of them.

"Dan," Socrates continued, "just look at yourself. If you remain blind to your weaknesses, how can you correct them?"

I could hardly speak. When I did, my voice quavered with anger and self-pity. "I *am* looking...." I didn't want to play the fool in front of her.

Blithely, Socrates went on. "Your slavish obedience to the

mind's moods and impulses is a serious error. If you persist, you'll remain yourself — and I can't imagine a worse fate." Socrates laughed heartily at this, and Joy nodded approvingly.

"He can be stuffy, can't he?" she said to Socrates.

I clenched my fists and kept my voice tightly controlled. "I don't find either of you amusing."

Socrates leaned back in his chair. "You're angry, but doing a mediocre job of hiding it. And your anger is proof of your stubborn illusions. Why defend a self you don't even believe in? When is the young jackass going to grow up?"

"You're the crazy one!" I heard myself scream. "I was fine until I met *you*. *Your* world seems full of suffering, not mine. I'm depressed all right, but only when I'm here with you!"

Neither Joy nor Socrates said a word. They just nodded their heads, looking sympathetic and compassionate. Damn their compassion! "You both think everything is so clear and so simple and so funny. I don't understand either one of you and I don't want to."

Blind with shame and confusion, feeling like a fool, I lurched out the door, swearing to myself that I would forget him, forget her, and forget I had ever walked into that station late one starry night.

My indignation was a sham, and I knew it. What was worse, I knew they knew it. I'd blown it. I felt like a small boy. I could bear looking stupid in front of Socrates, but not in front of Joy. And now I felt sure I'd lost her forever.

Running through the streets, I found myself going in the opposite direction from home. I ended up in a bar on University Avenue, near Grove Street. I got as drunk as I could, and when I finally made it to my apartment, I was grateful for unconsciousness.

I could never go back. I decided to try and take up the normal life I'd tossed aside months ago. The first thing was to catch up in my studies if I was to graduate. Susie loaned me her history notes, and I got psychology notes from one of my teammates. I stayed up late writing papers; I drowned myself in books. I had a lot to remember — and a lot to forget.

At the gym, I trained to exhaustion. At first my coach and

teammates were delighted to see this new energy. Rick and Sid, my two closest workout buddies, were amazed at my daring and joked about "Dan's death wish"; I attempted any move, ready or not. They thought I was bursting with courage, but I just didn't care — injury would at least give me a reason for the ache inside.

After a while, Rick and Sid's jokes stopped. "Dan, you're getting circles under your eyes. When's the last time you shaved?" Rick asked.

"You look — I don't know — too lean," said Sid.

"That's my business," I snapped. "No, I mean, thanks, but I'm fine, really."

"Well, get some sleep now and then, anyway, or there'll be nothing left of you by summer."

"Yeah, sure thing." I didn't tell them that I wouldn't mind disappearing.

I turned what few ounces of fat I had left into gristle and muscle. I looked hard, like one of Michelangelo's statues. My skin shone pale, translucent, like marble.

I went to movies almost every night but couldn't get the image of Socrates sitting in the station, maybe with Joy, out of my mind. Sometimes I had a dark vision of them both sitting there, laughing at me; maybe I was their warrior's quarry.

I didn't spend time with Susie or any of the other women I knew. What sexual urges I had were spent in training, washed away by sweat. Besides, how could I look into other eyes now that I had gazed into Joy's? One night, awakened by a knock, I heard Susie's timid voice outside. "Danny, are you in? Dan?" She slid a note under the door. I didn't even get up to look at the note.

My life became an ordeal. Other people's laughter hurt my ears. I imagined Socrates and Joy, cackling like warlock and witch, plotting against me. The movies I sat through had lost their colors; the food I ate tasted like paste. And one day in class, as Watson was analyzing social influences of something or other, I stood up and heard myself yell, "Bullshit!" at the top of my lungs. Watkins tried to ignore me, but all eyes, about 500 pairs, were on me. An audience. I'd show them! "Bullshit!" I yelled. A few anonymous hands clapped, and there was a smattering of laughter and whispering.

Watkins, never one to lose his tweed-suited cool, suggested, "Would you care to explain that?"

I pushed my way out of my seat to the aisle and walked up to the stage, suddenly wishing I'd shaved or worn a clean shirt. I stood facing him. "What has any of this stuff got to do with happiness, with life?" More applause from the audience. I could tell he was sizing me up to see if I was dangerous — and decided I might be. Damn straight! I was getting more confident.

"Perhaps you have a point," he acquiesced softly. I was being patronized in front of 500 people. I wanted to explain to them how it was — I would teach them, make them all see. I turned to the class and started to tell them about my meeting a man in a gas station who had shown me that life was not what it seemed. I started on the tale of the king on the mountain, lonely amid a town gone mad. At first, there was dead silence; then, a few people began laughing. What was wrong? I hadn't said anything funny. I went on with the story, but soon a wave of laughter spread through the auditorium. Were they all crazy, or was I?

Watkins whispered something to me, but I didn't hear. I went on pointlessly. He whispered again. "Son, I think they're laughing because your fly is open." Mortified, I glanced down and then out at the crowd. No! No, not again, not the fool again! Not the jackass again! I began to cry, and the laughter died.

I ran out of the hall and through the campus until I could run no more. Two women walked by me — to me they looked like plastic robots, social drones. They stared at me with distaste, then turned away.

I looked down at my dirty clothes, which probably smelled. My hair was matted and uncombed; I hadn't shaved in days. I found myself in the student union without remembering how I got there, and slumped into a sticky, plastic-covered chair and fell asleep. I dreamed I was impaled on a wooden horse by a gleaming sword. The horse, affixed to a tilting carousel, whirled round and round while I desperately reached out for the ring.

Melancholy music played off-key, and behind the music I heard a terrible laugh. I awoke, dizzy, and stumbled home.

I'd begun to drift through the routine of school like a phantom. My world was turning inside out and upside down. I had tried to rejoin the old ways I knew, to motivate myself in my studies and training, but nothing made sense anymore.

Meanwhile, professors rattled on and on about the Renaissance, the instincts of the rat, and Milton's middle years. I walked through Sproul Plaza each day amid campus demonstrations and walked through sit-ins as if in a dream; none of it meant anything to me. Student power gave me no comfort; drugs could give me no solace. So I drifted, a stranger in a strange land, caught between two worlds without a handhold on either.

Late one afternoon I sat in a redwood grove near the bottom of campus, waiting for the darkness, thinking about the best way to kill myself. I no longer belonged on this earth. Somehow I'd lost my shoes; I had on one sock, and my feet were brown with dried blood. I felt no pain, nothing.

I decided to see Socrates one last time. I shuffled toward the station and stopped across the street. He was finishing with a car as a lady and a little girl, about four years old, walked into the station. I don't think the woman knew Socrates; she could have been asking directions. Suddenly the little girl reached up to him. He lifted her and she threw her arms around his neck. The woman tried to pull the girl away from Socrates, but she wouldn't let go. Socrates laughed and talked to her, setting her down gently. He knelt down and they hugged each other.

I became unaccountably sad then, and started to cry. My body shook with anguish. I turned, ran a few hundred yards, and collapsed on the path. I was too weary to go home, to do anything; maybe that's what saved me.

I awoke in the infirmary. There was an IV needle in my arm. Someone had shaved me and cleaned me up. I felt rested, at least. I was released the next afternoon and called Cowell Health Center. "Dr. Baker, please." His secretary answered.

"My name is Dan Millman. I'd like to make an appointment with Dr. Baker as soon as possible."

"Yes, Mr. Millman," she said in the bright, professionally friendly voice of a psychiatrist's secretary. "The doctor has an opening a week from this Tuesday at 1 P.M.; would that be all right?"

"Isn't there anything sooner?"

"I'm afraid not...."

"I'm going to kill myself before a week from this Tuesday, lady."

"Can you come in this afternoon?" Her voice was soothing. "Will 2 P.M. be all right?"

"Yes."

"Fine, see you then, Mr. Millman."

Doctor Baker was a tall, corpulent man with a slight nervous tic around his left eye. Suddenly I didn't feel like talking to him at all. How would I begin? "Well, Herr Doktor. I have a teacher named Socrates who jumps up on rooftops — no, not off of them, that's what I'm planning to do. And, oh yes — he takes me on journeys to other places and times and I become the wind and I'm a little depressed and, yes school's fine and I'm a gymnastics star and I want to kill myself."

I stood. "Thank you for your time, doctor. I'm suddenly feeling great. I just wanted to see how the better half lived. It's been swell."

He started to speak, searching for the "right" thing to say, but I walked out, went home, and slept. For the time being, sleep seemed the easiest alternative.

That night, I dragged myself to the station. Joy was not there. Part of me suffered exquisite disappointment — I wanted so much to look into her eyes again, to hold her and be held — but part of me was relieved. It was one-on-one again — Soc and me.

When I sat down he said nothing of my absence, only, "You look tired and depressed." He said it without a trace of pity. My eyes filled with tears.

"Yes, I'm depressed. I came to say good-bye. I owe you that. I'm stuck halfway, and I can't stand it anymore. I don't want to live."

"You're wrong about two things, Dan." He came over and sat beside me on the couch. "First, you're not halfway yet, not by a long shot. But you are very close to the end of the tunnel. And the second thing," he said, reaching for my temples, "is that you're not going to kill yourself."

I glared at him. "Says who?" Then I realized we were no longer in the office, we were sitting in a cheap hotel room. There was no mistaking the musty smell, the thin, gray carpets, the two tiny beds, and the small, cracked secondhand mirror.

"What's going on?" For the moment, the life was back in my voice. These journeys were always a shock to my system; I felt a rush of energy.

"A suicide attempt is in progress. Only you can stop it."

"I'm not trying to kill myself just yet," I said.

"Not you, fool The young man outside the window, on the ledge. He's attending the University of Southern California. His name is Donald; he plays soccer and he's a philosophy major. He's in his senior year and he doesn't want to live. Go to it." Socrates gestured toward the window.

"Socrates, I can't."

"Then he'll die."

I looked out the window and saw, about fifteen stories below, groups of tiny people looking up from the streets of downtown Los Angeles. Peeking around the side of the window, I saw a light-haired young man in brown Levi's and a T-shirt standing ten feet away on the narrow ledge, looking down. He was getting ready to jump.

Not wanting to startle him, I called his name softly. He didn't hear me; I called again. "Donald."

He jerked his head up and almost fell. "Don't come near me!" he warned. Then, "How do you know my name?"

"A friend of my mine knows you, Donald. May I sit on the ledge here and talk to you? I won't come any closer."

"No, no more words." His face was lax, his monotone voice had already lost its life.

"Don — do people call you Don?"

"Yeah," he answered automatically.

"OK, Don, I guess it's your life. Anyway, 99 percent of the people in the world kill themselves."

"What the hell is that supposed to mean?" he said, an edge of life coming back into his voice. He started gripping the wall more tightly.

"Well, I'll tell you. The way most people *live* kills them — you know what I mean? They may take thirty or forty years to kill themselves by smoking or drinking or stress or overeating, but they kill themselves just the same."

I edged a few feet closer. I had to choose my words carefully. "My name is Dan. I wish we could spend more time talking; we might have some things in common. I'm an athlete, too, up at U.C. Berkeley."

"Well..." he stopped and started to shake.

"Listen, Don, it's getting a little scary for me to sit here on this ledge. I'm going to stand up so I can hold on to something." I stood slowly. I was shaking a little myself. "Jesus," I thought. "What am I doing out on this ledge?"

I spoke softly, trying to find a bridge to him. "I hear there's going to be a beautiful sunset tonight; the Santa Ana winds are blowing some storm clouds in. Are you sure you never want to see another sunset, or sunrise? Are you sure you never want to go hiking in the mountains again?"

"I've never been up to the mountains."

"You wouldn't believe it, Don. Everything is pure up there — the water, the air. You can smell pine needles everywhere. Maybe we could go hiking together. What do you think? Hell, if you want to kill yourself, you can always do it after you've at least seen the mountains."

There — I'd said all I could say. Now it was up to him. As I talked, I'd wanted more and more for him to live. I was only a few feet from him now.

"Stop!" he said. "I want to die...now."

I gave up. "All right," I said. "Then I'm going with you. I've already seen the goddamn mountains anyway."

He looked at me for the first time. "You're serious, aren't you?"

"Yeah, I'm serious. Are you going first, or am I?"

"But," he said, "why do you want to die? It's crazy. You look so healthy — you must have a lot to live for."

64

"Look," I said. "I don't know what your troubles are, but my problems dwarf yours; you couldn't even begin to grasp them. I'm through talking."

I looked down. It would be so easy: just lean out and let gravity do the rest. And for once, I'd prove smug old Socrates wrong. I could exit laughing, yelling, "You were wrong, you old bastard!" all the way down, until I smashed my bones and crushed my organs and cut myself off from the coming sunsets forever.

"Wait!" Don was reaching out for me. I hesitated, then grasped his hand. As I looked into his eyes, his face began to change. It narrowed. His hair grew darker, his body grew smaller. I was standing there, looking at myself. Then the mirror image disappeared, and I was alone.

Startled, I took a step backward and slipped. I fell, tumbling over and over. In my mind's eye, I saw the terrible hooded specter waiting expectantly below. I heard Soc's voice yelling from somewhere above, "Tenth floor, lingerie, bedspreads — eighth floor, housewares, cameras."

I was lying on the office couch, looking into Soc's gentle smile.

"Well?" he said. "Are you going to kill yourself?"

"No." But with that decision, the weight and responsibility of my life once again fell upon me. I told him how I felt. Socrates grasped my shoulders, and only said, "Stay with it, Dan."

Before I left that night, I asked him, "Where is Joy? I want to see her again."

"In good time. She'll come to you, later perhaps."

"But if I could only talk to her it would make things so much easier."

"Who ever told you it would be easy?"

"Socrates," I said, "I have to see her!"

"You don't have to do *anything* except to stop seeing the world from the viewpoint of your own personal cravings. Loosen up! When you lose your mind, you'll come to your senses. Until then, however, I want you to continue to observe, as much as possible, the debris of your mind."

"If I could just call her..."

"Get to it!" he said.

In the following weeks, the noise in my mind reigned supreme. Wild, random, stupid thoughts; guilts, anxieties, cravings — noise. Even in sleep, the deafening soundtrack of my dreams assaulted my ears. Socrates had been right all along. I *was* in prison.

It was a Tuesday night when I ran to the station at ten o'clock. Bursting into the office, I moaned, "Socrates! I'm going to go mad if I can't turn down the noise! My mind is wild — it's everything you told me!"

"Very good!" he said. "The first realization of a warrior."

"If this is progress, I want to regress."

"Dan, when you get on a wild horse that you believe is tame, what happens?"

"It throws you — or kicks your teeth in."

"Life has, in its own amusing way, kicked your teeth in many times."

I couldn't deny it. Not anymore.

"But when you *know* the horse is wild, you can deal with it appropriately."

"I think I understand, Socrates."

"Don't you mean you understand you think?" he smiled.

I left with instructions to let my "realization stabilize" for a few more days. I did my best. My awareness had grown these past few months, but I entered the office with the same questions: "Socrates, I've finally realized the extent of my mental noise; my horse is wild — how do I tame it? How do I turn down the noise? What can I do?"

He scratched his head. "Well, I guess you're just going to have to develop a very good sense of humor." He bellowed with laughter, then yawned and stretched — not the way most people usually do, with arms extended out to the side, but just like a cat. He rounded his back, and I heard his spine go crack-crack-crack-crack.

"Socrates, did you know that you looked just like a cat when you stretched?"

"I suppose I do," he replied nonchalantly. "It's a good

practice to copy the positive traits of various animals, just as we might imitate positive qualities of some humans. I happen to admire the cat; it moves like a warrior.

"And as it happens, you have modeled yourself after the jackass. It's time you started to expand your repertoire, don't you think?"

"Yes, I suppose it is," I answered calmly. But I was angry. I excused myself and went home early, just after midnight, and slept for five hours before my alarm woke me and I doubled back toward the station.

At that moment, I made a secret resolution. No more playing victim, someone he could feel superior to. I was going to be the hunter; I was going to stalk him.

It was still an hour until dawn, when his shift would end. I hid in the bushes that lined the bottom edge of campus, near the station. I would follow him and somehow find Joy.

Peering through the foliage, I watched his every move. My thoughts quieted in the intensity of my vigil. My sole desire was to find out about his life away from the station — a subject about which he'd always been silent. Now I'd track down the answers myself.

Like an owl I stared at him. I saw as never before how gracefully he moved. Like a cat. He washed windows without a wasted movement, slipped the nozzle into the gas tank like an artist.

Socrates went into the garage, probably to work on a car. I grew weary. The sky was already light when I roused myself from what must have been a few minutes of shut-eye. Oh, no — I'd missed him!

Then I saw him, busy with his last-minute duties. My heart constricted as he walked out of the station, crossed the street, and headed directly to where I sat — stiff, shivering, and achy, but well hidden. I just hoped he didn't feel like "beating around the bush" this morning.

I faded back into the foliage and calmed my breathing. A pair of sandals glided past, no more than four feet from my temporary lair. I could barely hear his soft footsteps. He followed a path that forked right.

Quickly but cautiously I scampered along the path like a squirrel. Socrates walked at a surprising clip. I barely kept up with his long strides and nearly lost him, when, far ahead, I saw a head of white hair entering Doe Library. What, I thought, could he be doing there of all places? Tingling with excitement, I closed in.

Once past the large oak door, I cut past a group of early-bird students who turned and laughed, watching me. I ignored them as I tracked my prey down a long corridor. I saw him turn right and disappear. I sprinted over to where he had vanished. There could be no mistake. He had entered this door. It was the men's room, and there was no other exit.

I didn't dare go in. I stationed myself in a nearby phone booth. Ten minutes passed; twenty minutes. Could I have missed him? My bladder was sending out emergency signals. I had to go in — not only to find Socrates, but to make use of the facilities. And why not? This was my domain after all, not his. I would make him explain. Still, it would be awkward.

Entering the tiled bathroom, I saw no one at first. After finishing my own business, I started to search more carefully. There was no other door, so he still had to be there. One guy came out of a stall and saw me hunched over, looking under the stalls. He hurried out the door with wrinkled brow, shaking his head.

Back to the business at hand. I ducked my head for a quick look under the last stall. First I saw the backs of a pair of sandaled feet, then suddenly Soc's face dropped into view, upside down with a lopsided grin. He obviously had his back to the door and was bending forward, his head down between his knees.

I stumbled backward in shock, completely disoriented. I had no good reason for my bizarre bathroom behavior.

Socrates swung the stall door open and flushed with a flourish, "Whoooeee, a man can get constipated when he's being stalked by a junior warrior!" As his laughter thundered through the tiled room, I reddened. He'd done it again! I could almost feel my ears lengthen as I was once again transformed into a jackass. My body churned with a mixture of shame and anger.

I could feel my face turn red. I glanced at the mirror, and there, tied neatly in my hair, was a perky yellow ribbon. Things began to make sense: the people's smiles and laughter as I'd walked through campus, the strange look I'd gotten from my fellow bathroom occupant. Socrates must have affixed it to my head while I dozed off in the bushes. Suddenly very tired, I turned and walked out the door.

Just before it swung shut, I heard Socrates say, not without a tone of sympathy in his voice, "That was just to remind you who is the teacher and who is the student."

That afternoon, I trained like the unleashed furies of hell. I talked to no one, and wisely, no one said a word to me. I quietly raged and swore I'd do whatever was necessary to make Socrates acknowledge me as a warrior.

One of my teammates stopped me on my way out and handed me an envelope. "Someone left this in the coach's office. It's addressed to you, Dan. A fan of yours?"

"I don't know. Thanks, Herb."

I stepped outside the door and ripped open the envelope. On an unlined piece of paper was written: "Anger is stronger than fear, stronger than sorrow. Your spirit is growing. You are ready for the sword — Socrates."

CHAPTER THREE

CUTTING FREE

The next morning, fog had rolled in off the bay, covering the summer sun, chilling the air. I awoke late, made some tea, ate an apple, pulled out my small TV, and dumped some cookies into a bowl. Switching on a soap opera, I immersed myself in someone else's problems. As I watched, mesmerized by the drama, I reached for another cookie and discovered that the bowl was empty. Could I have eaten all those cookies?

Later that morning, I went running around Edwards Field. There I met Dwight, who worked up at the Lawrence Hall of Science in the Berkeley hills. I had to ask his name a second time, because I "didn't catch it" the first time, another reminder of my lack of attention and wandering mind. After a few laps, Dwight remarked about the cloudless blue sky. But lost in thought, I hadn't even noticed the sky. Then he headed for the hills — he was a marathon runner — and I returned home, thinking about my mind — a self-defeating activity if ever there was one.

I observed that in the gym I kept my attention focused precisely on every action, but when I stopped soaring, my thoughts would again obscure my perception.

That night I walked to the station early, hoping to greet Socrates at the beginning of his shift. By now I'd done my best to forget about yesterday's incident in the library and was ready to hear any antidote to my hyperactive mind that Soc cared to suggest.

I waited. Midnight arrived. Soon after, so did Socrates.

We had just settled into the office when I started to sneeze and had to blow my nose. I had a slight cold. Soc put the tea-kettle on, and I began, as was my custom, with a question.

"Socrates, how do I stop my thoughts, my mind — other than by developing a sense of humor?"

"First you need to understand where your thoughts come from, how they arise in the first place. For example, you have a cold now; its physical symptoms tell you when your body needs to rebalance itself, to restore its proper relationship with sunlight, fresh air, simple food. Just so, stressful thoughts reflect a conflict with reality. Stress happens when the mind resists what is."

A car rolled into the station bearing a formally dressed older couple who sat like two ramrods in the front seat. "Come with me," Soc ordered. He removed his windbreaker and his cotton sport shirt, revealing a bare chest and shoulders with lean, well-defined muscles under smooth, translucent skin.

He walked up to the driver's side of the car and smiled at the shocked pair. "What can I do for you folks? Gasoline to fuel your spirits? Perhaps oil to smooth out the rough spots in your day? How about a new battery to put a little charge in your life?" He winked at them openly and stood his ground, smiling, as the car lurched forward and sped away from the station. He scratched his head. "Maybe they just remembered that they left the water running at home."

While we relaxed in the office, sipping our tea, Socrates explained his lesson. "You saw that man and woman resist what to them represented a strange situation. Conditioned by their values and fears, they haven't learned to cope with spon-taneity. I could have been the highlight of their day.

"You see, Dan, when you resist what happens, your mind begins to race; the thoughts that assail you are actually created by you."

"And your mind works differently?"

"Yes and no. My mind is like a pond without ripples. Your

mind is full of waves because you feel separated from, and often threatened by, an unplanned, unwelcome occurrence. Your mind is like a pond into which someone has just dropped a boulder!"

As I listened, I gazed into the depths of my teacup, when I felt a touch just behind the ears. Suddenly my attention intensified; I had stared deeper and deeper into the cup, down, down...

I was underwater, looking up. This was ridiculous! Had I fallen into my teacup? I had fins and gills; very fishy. I whipped my tail and darted to the bottom, where it was silent and peaceful.

Suddenly a huge rock crashed into the water's surface. Shock waves slapped me backward. My fins whipped the water again and I took off, seeking shelter. I hid until everything quieted down again. As time passed, I became accustomed to the little stones that sometimes fell into the water, making ripples. The large plunks, however, still startled me.

In a world filled with sound and dryness again, I lay on the couch, looking up, wide-eyed, at Soc's smile.

"Socrates, that was incredible!"

"Please, not another fish story. I'm glad you had a nice swim. Now, may I continue?" He didn't wait for an answer.

"You were a very nervous fish, fleeing every large ripple. Later, you became used to the ripples but still had no insight into their cause. You can see," he continued, "that a magnificent leap of awareness is required for the fish to extend its vision beyond the water in which it is immersed to the source of the ripples.

"A similar leap of awareness will be required of you. When you understand the source clearly, you'll see that the ripples of your mind have nothing to do with you; you'll just watch them, without attachment, no longer compelled to overreact every time a pebble drops. You will be free of the world's turbulence as soon as you stop taking your thoughts so seriously.

Remember — when you are in trouble, let go of your thoughts to see through your mind!"

"Socrates, how?"

"A not-so-bad question. As you've learned from your physical training, leaps of awareness don't happen all at once; they require time and practice. And the practice of insight into the source of your own ripples is meditation."

With that grand announcement, he excused himself and went to the bathroom. Now it was time to spring my surprise on him. I yelled from the couch, so he could hear me through the bathroom door. "I'm one step ahead of you, Socrates. I joined a meditation group a week ago. I thought I'd do something myself about this old mind of mine," I explained. "And I'm already starting to relax more and get some control over my thoughts. Have you noticed I've been calmer? In fact — "

The bathroom door blasted open and Socrates came straight at me, screaming a bloodcurdling shriek, holding a gleaming samurai sword over his head! Before I could move, the sword slashed at me, cutting silently through the air, and stopped inches over my head. I looked up at the hovering sword, then at Socrates. He grinned at me.

"What the hell! You scared the shit out of me!" I gasped.

The blade ascended slowly. Poised over my head, it seemed to capture and intensify all the light in the room. It shone in my eyes and made me squint. I decided to shut up.

Socrates knelt on the floor in front of me, gently placed the sword between us, closed his eyes, took a deep breath, and sat perfectly still. I watched him for a while, wondering if this "sleeping tiger" would waken and leap at me if I moved. Ten minutes passed, then twenty. I figured maybe he wanted me to meditate, too, so I closed my eyes and sat for half an hour. Opening my eyes, I watched him still sitting there like a Buddha. I started to fidget and got up quietly to get a drink of water. I was filling my mug when he put his hand on my shoulder. Water sloshed over my shoes as my hand jerked.

"Socrates, I wish you wouldn't sneak up on me like that. Couldn't you make some noise?"

He smiled, and spoke. "Silence is the warrior's art — and

meditation is his sword. With it, you'll cut through your illusions. But understand this: the sword's usefulness depends upon the swordsman. If you don't know how to use the weapon properly, it can become a dangerous, deluding, or useless tool. Meditation can initially help you to relax. You may put your 'sword' on display, proudly show it to friends. The gleam of this sword distracts many meditators until they abandon it to seek other esoteric techniques.

"In contrast, the warrior uses the sword of meditation with skill and understanding. With it, he cuts the mind to ribbons, slashing through thoughts to reveal their lack of substance. Maybe you recall the story of Alexander the Great, marching with his armies through the desert and coming upon two thick ropes tied in the massive, convoluted Gordian knot. No one had ever been able to untie it. Without a moment's hesitation Alexander drew his sword and, in one powerful blow, sliced the knot in two. This is the warrior's way of meditation. And this is how you must learn to attack the knots of your mind. Until one day you transcend your need for any weapon at all."

Just then an old VW bus with a new coat of white paint and a rainbow painted on its side chugged into the station. Inside sat six people, hard to tell apart. As we approached them, we could see that there were two women and four men, all dressed from head to toe in the same blue outfits. I recognized them as members of one of the many new spiritual groups in the Bay Area. These particular people self-righteously avoided acknowledging our presence, as if our worldliness might contaminate them.

Socrates, of course, rose to the challenge, immediately affecting a combination limp and lisp persona. Scratching himself profusely, he was the perfect Quasimodo. "Hey, Jack," he said to the driver, who had the longest beard I'd ever seen, "ya want gas, or what?"

"Yes, we want gas," the man said, his voice as smooth as olive oil.

Socrates leered at the two women in the back and, sticking his head in the window, he whispered loudly, "Hey do you *meditate?"* He said it as if he were referring to a solitary form of sexual release.

"Yes, we do," said the driver, cosmic superiority oozing from his voice. "Now, will you put gas in our vehicle?"

Soc waved at me to fill the tank, while he proceeded to push every button the driver had. "Hey, ya know, you look kinda like a girl in that dress, guy — don't get me wrong, it's real pretty. And why don't you shave; what are ya hiding under that fuzz?"

While I cringed, he went from bad to even worse. "Hey," he said to one of the women, "is this guy your boyfriend? Tell me," he said to the other man in the front seat, "do you ever do it, or do you save it up like I read in the *National Enquirer?"*

That about did it. By the time Socrates counted out their change — with agonizing slowness — he kept losing count and starting over — I was ready to burst out laughing and the people in the van were trembling with anger. The driver grabbed his change and drove out of the station in a very unsaintly way. As their van pulled out, Socrates yelled, "I hear meditation is good for you. Keep practicing!"

We'd no sooner returned to the office when a big Chevy pulled into the station. The clang of the business bell was followed by an impatient "ooga-ooga" from a musical horn. I went out with Socrates to help.

Behind the wheel sat a forty-year-old "teenager" dressed in flashy satin clothes topped with a large feathered safari hat. He was extremely jittery and kept tapping the steering wheel. Next to him, batting false eyelashes in the rearview mirror as she powdered her nose, sat a woman of indeterminate age.

For some reason, they offended me. They looked asinine. I wanted to say, "Why don't you act your age?" but I watched and waited.

"Hey man, ya got a cigarette machine here?" the hyperactive driver said.

Socrates stopped what he had been doing and with a warm smile said, "No, sir, but there's an all-night market down the road." Then he returned to checking the oil, giving it his full attention. He returned the change as if he were serving tea to the emperor.

After the car sped away we remained at the pump, smelling the night air. "You treated these people so courteously but were positively obnoxious to our blue-robed seekers, who were obviously on a higher evolutionary level. What's the story?"

For once, he gave me a simple, direct answer. "The only levels that should concern you are mine — and yours," he said with a grin. "These people needed kindness. The spiritual seekers needed something else to reflect upon."

"What do I need?" I blurted.

"More practice," he answered quickly. "Your practice didn't help you stay calm when I ran at you with the sword, nor did it help our blue-robed friends when I poked a little fun at them.

"Let me put it this way: A forward roll is not the whole of gymnastics. A meditation technique is not the whole of the warrior's way. If you fail to understand the complete picture, you might be deluded, practicing only forward rolls — or only meditation — your whole life, thus reaping only fragmented benefits of training.

"What you need is a map of the entire terrain you need to explore. Then you'll realize the uses, and the limits, of meditation. And I ask you, where can you get a good map?"

"At a service station, of course."

"Right you are, sir. Just step into the office. I have just the map you need." We entered laughing, through the garage door. I plopped onto the couch; Socrates settled without a sound between the massive armrests of his plush chair.

He stared at me for a full minute. I started getting goose bumps. "Uh-oh," I said nervously under my breath. "What's up?"

"The problem is," he sighed at last, "that I can't describe the terrain for you, at least not in so many...words." He rose and walked toward me with that shine in his eye that told me to pack my suitcases — I was going on a trip.

For an instant, from a vantage point somewhere in space, I felt myself expanding at the speed of light, ballooning, exploding to the outermost limits of existence until I *was* the universe. Nothing separate remained. I had become everything. I was Consciousness, recognizing itself; I was the pure light that physicists equate with all matter, and poets define as love. I was one, and I was all, outshining all the worlds. In that moment, the eternal, the unknowable had been revealed to me as an indescribable certainty.

In a flash, I was back in my mortal form, floating among the stars. I saw a prism shaped like a human heart, which dwarfed every galaxy. It diffracted the light of consciousness into an explosion of radiant colors, sparkling splinters of every rainbow hue, spreading throughout the cosmos.

My own body became a radiant prism, throwing splinters of multicolored light everywhere. And it came to me that the highest purpose of the human body is to become a clear channel for this light — so that its brightness can dissolve all obstructions, all knots, all resistance.

I felt the light diffracted across the systems of my own body. Then I knew that awareness is how the human being experiences the light of consciousness.

I learned the meaning of attention — it is the intentional channeling of awareness. I felt my body again, as a hollow vessel. I looked at my legs; they filled with warm, radiant light, disappearing into brightness. I looked at my arms, with the same result. I focused attention on every part of the body, until I became wholly light once again. Finally, I realized the process of real meditation — to expand awareness, to direct attention, to ultimately surrender to the light of consciousness.

A light flickered in darkness. I awoke to Socrates shining a flashlight back and forth across my eyes. "Power failure," he said, baring his teeth like a Halloween pumpkin as he held the light up to his face. "Well, is it all a bit clearer now?" he asked, as if I had just learned how a lightbulb worked, rather than seen the soul of the universe. I could hardly speak.

"Socrates, I owe you a debt that I can never repay. I understand everything now, and I know what I must do. I don't suppose I'll be needing to see you again." I was sad that I had graduated. I would miss him.

He looked at me, a startled expression on his face, then started to laugh more uproariously than I'd ever seen before. He shook all over; tears ran down his cheeks. Finally he calmed and explained his laughter. "You haven't quite graduated, junior; your work has hardly begun. Look at yourself. You are fundamentally the same as when you stumbled in here months ago. What you saw was only a vision, not a conclusive experience. It will fade into memory, but even so, it will serve as a reminder and reference point. Now relax and stop acting so serious!"

He sat back, as mischievous and wise as ever. "You see," he added, "these little journeys do save me some difficult explanations I must go through to enlighten you." Just then, the lights flashed on, and we laughed.

Smiling, he reached into his small refrigerator next to the water cooler and brought out some oranges, which he started to squeeze into juice as he continued. "If you must know, you're doing me a service, too. I'm also 'stuck' in a place in time and space, and owe a kind of debt myself. A lot of me is tied up with your progress. In order to teach you," he said, tossing the orange rinds back over his shoulder into the wastebasket, making a perfect shot every time, "I literally had to put a part of me in you. Quite an investment, I assure you. So it's a team effort all the way."

He finished the juice and handed me a small glassful. "A toast then," I said, "to a successful partnership."

"Done," he smiled.

"Tell me more about this debt. To whom do you owe it?"

"Let's say that it's part of the House Rules."

"That's no answer at all."

"Silly it may be, but still I must abide by a particular set of rules in my business." He took out a small card. It looked normal enough, until I noticed a faint glow. In embossed letters, it said,

Warrior, Inc.
Socrates, Prop.
Specializing in:
Paradox, Humor,
and Change

"Keep it safe. Someday it may come in handy. When you need me — when you really need me — just hold the card in both hands and call. I'll be there, one way or another."

I put the card carefully in my wallet. "I'll keep it safe, Socrates. You can count on it. Uh, by the way, you wouldn't have one of those cards with Joy's address on it, would you?"

He ignored me.

We were silent then, as Socrates began to prepare one of his crisp salads. Then I thought of another question. "So, how do I do it? How do I open myself to this light of awareness?"

Answering my question with a question, he asked, "what do you do when you want to see?"

I laughed. "Well, I look! You mean meditation?"

"Here's the core of it," he said suddenly as he sliced and diced the vegetables. "Meditation consists of two simultaneous processes: One is *insight* — paying attention to what is arising. The other is *surrender* — letting go of attachment to arising thoughts. This is how you cut free of the mind."

"I think I know what you mean."

"Well, maybe you've heard the story about a student of meditation who was sitting in deep silence with a small group of practitioners. Terrified by a vision of blood, death, and demons, he got up, walked to the teacher, and whispered, '*Roshi*, I've just had a horrible vision!' 'Let it go,' said his teacher. A few days later, the student was enjoying erotic fantasies, insights into the meaning of life, and visions of angels — the works. Just then, his teacher came up behind him with a stick and whacked him, saying, 'Let it go!'"

I laughed at the story and said, "You know, Soc, I've been thinking..." Socrates gave me a whack on the head with a carrot, saying, "Let it go!"

We ate. I stabbed at my vegetables with a fork; he picked up each small bite with wooden chopsticks, breathing quietly as he chewed. He never picked up another bite until he was completely done with the first, as if each bite was a small meal in itself. I kind of admired the way he ate as I chomped merrily away. I finished first, sat back, and announced, "I guess I'm ready to have a go at real meditation."

"Ah, yes." He put down his chopsticks. "'Conquering the mind.' If only you were interested."

"I am interested! I want self-awareness. That's why I'm here."

"You want self-image, not self-awareness. You're here because you have no better alternatives."

"But I do want to get rid of my noisy mind," I protested.

"More illusion — like the man who refuses to wear glasses, insisting 'they aren't printing the newspapers clearly anymore.'"

"Wrong," I said, shaking my head back and forth.

"I don't really expect you to see the truth of it yet, but you need to hear it."

"What's your point?" I asked impatiently, my attention drifting outside.

"Here is the bottom line," Socrates said, in a voice that firmly held my attention. "You still believe that you are your thoughts and defend them as if they were treasures."

"No way. How can you know that?"

"Your stubborn illusions are a sinking ship, junior. I recommend that you let them go while there's still time."

I stifled my rising temper. "How can *you* know how I 'identify' with my mind?"

"OK," he sighed. "I'll prove it to you: what do you mean when you say, 'I'm going to my house'? Don't you naturally assume that you are separate from the house that you are going to?"

"Well, of course."

"Then what do you mean when you say, 'My body is sore today'? Who is the 'I' who is separate from the body and speaks of it as a possession?"

I had to laugh. "Semantics, Socrates. You have to say something."

"Yes — and the conventions of language reveal the ways we see the world. You do, in fact, act as if you were a 'mind' or a subtle something inside the body."

"Why would I possibly want to do that?"

"Because you fear death and crave survival. You want Forever, you desire Eternity. In your deluded belief that you are

81

this 'mind' or 'spirit' or 'soul,' you find the escape clause in your contract with mortality. Perhaps as 'mind' you can wing free of the body when it dies, hmm?"

"It's a thought," I said with a grin.

"That's exactly what it is, Dan — a thought — no more real than the shadow of a shadow. Consciousness is not *in* the body; the body is *in* Consciousness. And you *are* that Consciousness — not the phantom mind that troubles you so. You are the body, but you are everything else, too. That is what your vision revealed to you. Only the mind resists change. When you relax mindless into the body, you are happy and content and free, sensing no separation. Immortality is *already* yours, but not in the way you imagine or hope for. You have been immortal since before you were born and will be long after the body dissolves. The body is Consciousness; never born; never dies; only changes. The mind — your ego, personal beliefs, history, and identity — is all that ends at death. And who needs it?" Socrates leaned back into his chair.

"I'm not sure all of that sank in."

"Of course not." He laughed. "Words mean little unless you realize the truth of it yourself. And when you do, you'll be free at last."

"That sounds pretty good."

"Yes, I'd say it is pretty good. Right now I'm only laying the groundwork for what comes next."

I considered what he said for at least ten seconds before my next question erupted. "Socrates, if I'm not my thoughts, what am I?"

He looked at me as if he'd just finished explaining that one and one are two and I'd then asked, "Yes, but what are one and one?" He reached over to the refrigerator, grasped an onion, and tossed it to me. "Peel it, layer by layer," he demanded. I started peeling. "What do you find?"

"Another layer."

"Continue."

I peeled off a few more layers. "Just more layers, Soc."

"Keep going."

"There's nothing left."

"There's something left, all right."

"What's that?"

"The universe. Consider that as you walk home."

I looked out the window; it was almost dawn.

I returned the next night after a mediocre meditation session, still brimming with thoughts. There wasn't much business, so we sat back, sipping peppermint tea, and I told him about my lackluster meditation practice. He smiled and said, "Maybe you've heard about the Zen student who asked his teacher the most important element of Zen. The roshi replied, 'Attention.' 'Yes, thank you,' the student replied. 'But can you tell me the second most important element?' And the roshi replied, 'Attention.'"

Puzzled, I looked up at Soc, waiting for more. "That's all, folks," he said.

I stood up to get some water. Socrates asked, "Are you paying close attention to your standing?"

"Yeah, sure," I answered, not at all sure that I was. I walked over to the dispenser.

"Are you paying close attention to your walking?" he asked.

"Yes, I am," I answered, starting to catch on to the game.

"Are you paying attention to how your mouth shapes the words you say?"

"Well, I guess so," I said, listening to my voice. I was getting flustered.

"Are you paying attention to how you think?" he asked.

"Socrates, give me a break — I'm doing the best I can!"

He leaned toward me. "Your best is apparently not good enough. At least not yet. Your attention must *burn*. Aimlessly rolling around a gym mat doesn't develop a champion; sitting with your eyes closed and letting your mind wander doesn't train your attention. Focus! Do or die!" Soc smiled. "That reminds me of something that happened many years ago.

"In a monastery, I sat day after day, struggling with a koan — a riddle my teacher had given me in order to spur the mind to see its true nature. I couldn't solve it. Each time I went to the roshi, I had nothing to offer him. I was a slow student and was becoming discouraged. He told me to continue working on my koan for one more month. 'Surely then,' he encouraged me, 'you will solve it.'

"A month passed, and I tried my best. The koan remained a mystery. 'Stay with it one more week, with fire in your heart!' he told me. Day and night the koan burned, but still I could not see through it.

"My roshi told me, 'One more day, with all your spirit.' At the end of the day, I was exhausted. I told him, 'Master, it's no use — a month, a week, a day — I cannot pierce the riddle.' My teacher looked at me a long time. 'Meditate for one more hour,' he said. 'If you have not solved the koan by then, you had better kill yourself.'

"By the end of the hour, facing imminent death, my awareness broke through the mind's barriers."

"Why should a warrior sit around meditating?" I asked. "I thought the warrior's way was about action."

"Sitting meditation is the beginner's practice. Eventually, you will learn to meditate in every action. Sitting serves as a ceremony, a time to practice balance, ease, and divine detachment. Master the ritual before you expand the same insight and surrender fully into daily life.

"As your teacher, I will use every method and artifice at my command to help you persevere with the work ahead. If I had just walked up to you and told you the secret of happiness, you would not even have heard me. You needed someone to fascinate you, to appear to jump up on rooftops before you could get a little interested.

"Well, I'm willing to play games, for a little while at least, but there comes a time when every warrior must walk the path alone. For now, I'll do what is necessary to keep you here, learning this way."

I felt manipulated and angry. "So I can grow old sitting in this gas station like you, waiting to pounce on innocent students?" I regretted my remark as soon as it slipped out.

Socrates, unfazed, smiled and spoke. "Don't mistake this

place, or your teacher, Dan. Things and people are not always as they seem. I am defined by the universe, not by this station. As to why you should stay, well, that may become clear. I am completely happy, you see. Are you?"

A car pulled in, clouds of steam surrounding its radiator. "Come on," Soc said. "This car is suffering and we may have to shoot it and put it out of its misery." We both went out to the stricken car, whose radiator was boiling and whose owner was in a foul mood, fuming.

"What took you so long? I can't wait around here all night, damn it!"

Socrates looked at him with nothing less than loving compassion. "Let's see if we can't help you, sir, and make this only a minor inconvenience." He had the man drive into the garage, where he put a pressure cap on the radiator and found the leak. Within a few minutes he'd welded the hole shut but told the man that he would still need a new radiator in the near future. "Everything dies and changes, even radiators," he winked at me.

As the man drove away, the truth of Soc's words sank in. He really was completely happy! Nothing seemed to affect his happy mood. In all the time I'd known him, he had acted angry, sad, gentle, tough, humorous, and even concerned. But always, a kind of peace and happiness had shone in his eyes, even when they brimmed with tears.

I thought about Socrates as I walked home, my shadow growing and shrinking with each streetlight I passed. I kicked a stone into the darkness as I neared my apartment, walking softly down the driveway to the back, where my little converted garage waited under the branches of a walnut tree.

It was only a few hours away from dawn. I lay in bed but couldn't sleep, wondering whether I could discover his secret. It seemed even more important right now than jumping up onto rooftops.

Then I remembered the card he had given me. Quickly, I got out of bed and turned on the light. Reaching into my wallet, I extracted it. My heart started to beat rapidly. Socrates had said that if I ever really needed him, to hold the card in both hands and just call. Well, I was going to test him.

I stood for a moment, trembling; my knees were starting to shake. I took the softly glowing card in both hands and called, "Socrates, come in Socrates. Dan calling." I felt like a complete fool, standing there at 4:55 A.M., holding a glowing card, talking to the air. Nothing happened. I tossed it carelessly onto the dresser in disgust. That's when the light went out.

"What?" I yelled as I spun around trying to sense if he was there. In classic movie style, I took a step backward, tripped over my chair, bounced off the edge of the bed, and sprawled to the floor.

The light went back on. If someone had been within earshot, that person might have assumed I was a student having trouble with ancient Greek studies. Why else would I be yelling at 5:02 in the morning, "Damn it, Socrates!"

I'd never know whether the blackout had been a coincidence or not. Socrates had only said that he would come; he hadn't said in what form. I sheepishly picked up the card and started to slip it back into my wallet, when I noticed it had changed. Underneath the last lines, "Paradox, Humor, and Change," appeared two words in bold print: "Emergencies Only!"

Laughing, I fell asleep in no time at all.

Summer workouts had begun. It was good to see old familiar faces. Herb was growing a beard; Rick and Sid were cultivating their dark summer tans and looked slimmer and stronger than ever.

I wanted so much to share my life and the lessons I'd been learning with my teammates, but I didn't know where to begin. Then I remembered Soc's business card. Before warm-up began, I called Rick over. "Hey, I want to show you something." Once he saw that glowing card and Soc's "specialties," I knew he'd want to know more about it; maybe they all would.

After a dramatic pause, I pulled the card out and flipped it over to him. "Pretty strange, huh?"

Rick looked down at the card, turned it over, then looked

back up at me, his face as blank as the card. "Is this a joke? I don't get it, Dan."

I looked at the card, then turned it over. "Uh," I grunted, stuffing the piece of paper back into my wallet, "Wrong card. Never mind. Let's warm up." I sighed. Great — this would be sure to strengthen my reputation as the team eccentric.

What a cheap trick, I thought. Disappearing ink.

That night, I pulled the card out and threw it down on the desk. "I wish you'd quit the practical jokes, Socrates. I'm tired of looking like an idiot."

He looked at me sympathetically. "Oh? Have you been looking like an idiot again?"

"Socrates, come on. I'm asking you — will you please stop it?"

"Stop what?"

"The gag with the disappear — " Out of the corner of my eye I caught a soft glow from the vicinity of the desk:

> *Warrior, Inc.*
> *Socrates, Prop.*
> *Specializing in:*
> *Paradox, Humor,*
> *and Change.*
> **Emergencies Only!**

"I don't get it," I murmured. "Does this card change?"

"Everything changes," he replied.

"Yes, I know, but does it disappear and appear again?"

"Everything disappears and appears again."

"Socrates, when I showed it to Rick, there was nothing there."

"It's the House Rules," he shrugged, smiling.

"You're not being particularly helpful; I want to know how..."

"Let it go," he said. "Let it go."

Summer passed quickly, with intensive workouts and late nights with Socrates. We spent half the time practicing meditation and the other half working in the garage or just relaxing over tea. At times like these I would ask about Joy; I longed to see her again. Socrates would tell me nothing.

With vacation's end imminent, my mind drifted back to the coming classes. I had decided to fly down to L.A. for a week's visit with my parents. I would put my Valiant in garage storage here, and buy a motorcycle while down in L.A., then drive it up the coast.

I was walking down Telegraph Avenue to do some shopping and had just come out of the pharmacy with toothpaste when a scrawny teenager came up to me, so close I could smell stale alcohol and sweat. "Spare some change, can't you?" he asked, not looking at me.

"No, sorry," I said, not feeling sorry at all. As I walked away, I thought, "Get a job." Then vague guilts came into my mind; I'd said no to a penniless beggar. Angry thoughts arose. "He shouldn't walk up to people like that!"

I was halfway down the block before I realized all the mental noise I had tuned in to, and the tension it was causing — just because some guy had asked me for money and I'd said no. In that instant I let it go. Feeling lighter, I took a deep breath, shook off the tension, and turned my attention to the beautiful day.

That night at the station I told Socrates my news.

"Soc, I'm flying down to L.A. in a few days to visit my folks, maybe buy a motorcycle. Hey, and I just learned this afternoon that the U.S. Gymnastics Federation is flying Sid and me to Yugoslavia to train with the gymnasts competing in the World Gymnastics Championships. They think we're both potential Olympians and want us to get some exposure. How about that?"

To my surprise, Socrates frowned. "What will be, will be."

Feeling high, I chose to ignore this and started out the door. "Well, bye for now. See you in a few weeks."

"In a few hours," he responded. "Meet me at Ludwig's fountain. Noon."

Wondering what was up, I said good night.

I got six hours' sleep and ran to the fountain named after a dog who used to frequent the spot. Several canines were romping and splashing there, cooling off from the August heat; a few little kids were wading in the shallow water.

Just as the Campanile, Berkeley's famous bell tower, began to chime the noon hour, Soc's shadow appeared at my feet. "Let's walk," he said. We strolled up through campus, past Sproul Hall, beyond the optometry school and Cowell Hospital, up beyond the football stadium, into the hills of Strawberry Canyon.

Finally, he spoke. "For you, Dan, a conscious process of transformation has begun. There's no going back. To try and do so would end in... well, no sense talking about that. I need to know that you're committed."

"You mean like in an institution?" I tried to joke.

He grinned. "Something like that."

We walked silently after that, in the shade of the overgrown bushes along the running trail.

High above the city, Socrates spoke again. "No one can help you beyond a certain point, Dan. I'll be guiding you for a while, but then even I must step back, and you will be alone. You will be tested severely before it's done. You'll need great inner strength. I only hope it comes in time."

The mild bay breeze had stopped and the air was hot; still, I felt a chill. Shivering in the heat, I watched a lizard scurrying through the underbrush. Soc's last few words had just registered. I turned —

He was gone.

Frightened, without knowing why, I hurried back down the trail. I didn't know it then, but my preparations had ended. And my training was about to begin with an ordeal I almost didn't survive.

BOOK TWO

THE WARRIOR'S TRAINING

CHAPTER FOUR

THE SWORD IS SHARPENED

After storing my Valiant in a rented garage, I boarded the "F" bus to San Francisco, connecting with Airport Transit, which got caught in a traffic jam. It looked as if I'd be late for my flight. Anxious thoughts began to arise; I felt my belly tense — then, as soon as I noticed it, I let it all go as I'd been trained. I relaxed and enjoyed the scenery along Bayshore Freeway, reflecting on my growing mastery over stressful thoughts, which had habitually plagued me in the past. And as it turned out, I caught my plane with seconds to spare.

Dad, an older version of me with thinning hair, wearing a bright blue sport shirt over his muscular chest, met me at the airport with a strong handshake and a warm smile. Mom's face crinkled sweetly as she greeted me at the door of their apartment with hugs and kisses and news about my sister and nieces and nephews.

That evening I was treated to one of Mom's latest piano pieces — Bach, I think it was. The next morning at dawn, Dad and I were out on the golf course. All the while, I'd been tempted to tell them about my adventures with Socrates, but thought better of silence. Perhaps I'd explain it all in writing someday. It was good to visit home, but home now seemed so long ago and far away.

When Dad and I were sitting in the sauna at the gym after our golf game, he said, "Danny, college life must agree with

93

you. You seem different — more relaxed, nicer to be around — not that you weren't nice to be around before..." He was searching for the right words, but I understood.

I smiled. If he only knew.

A few days later, I found my motorcycle — a 500 cc Triumph. It took me a while to get comfortable with it. I almost fell twice, each time thinking I'd seen Joy coming out of a store or disappearing around a corner. I reminded myself to pay attention.

My final night in L.A. arrived; I took crash helmet in hand and left the house to shop for a new suitcase. I heard Dad call out, "Be careful, Dan, motorcycles are hard to see at night." His usual caution.

"Sure, Dad, I'll be careful," I yelled back. Then I gunned the bike and pulled out into the warm night air, wearing my gymnastics T-shirt, faded Levi's, and work boots. I felt on top of the world; there was so much to look forward to. My future was about to change, because at that moment, three blocks ahead, a man named George Wilson was preparing to make a left turn on Western Avenue.

I roared through the dusk; the streetlights flashed by as I approached Seventh and Western. I was about to enter the intersection when I noticed a white Cadillac facing me, signaling for a left turn. I slowed down — a small precaution that probably saved my life.

Just as my bike entered the intersection the Cadillac suddenly accelerated, turning directly in front of me. For a few more precious seconds, the body I was born with was still in one piece.

There was time enough to think, but not to act. "Cut left!" my mind screamed. But there was oncoming traffic. "Swerve right!" I'd never clear the fender. "Lay it down!" I'd slide under the wheels. My options were gone. I slammed on the brakes and waited. It was unreal, like a dream, until I saw a flashing image of the driver's horrified face. With a terrible thud and the musical sound of tinkling glass, my bike smashed into the car's front fender — and my right leg shattered. Then everything sped up horribly as the world turned black.

I must have lost consciousness just after my body somer-saulted over the car and crashed onto the concrete. I awoke to a moment of blessed numbness, then the pain began, like a searing, red-hot vise, squeezing and crushing my leg tighter and tighter until it became more than I could bear and I started to scream. I wanted it to stop; I prayed for unconsciousness. Faraway voices: "...just didn't see him..." "...parents' phone number..." "...take it easy, they'll be here soon."

Then I heard a faraway siren, and hands were removing my helmet, lifting me onto a stretcher. I looked down and saw the white bone sticking out through the torn leather of my boot. With the slam of the ambulance door, I suddenly recalled Soc's words, "...you will be tested severely before it's done."

Seconds later, it seemed, I was lying on the X-ray table in the emergency room of L.A. Orthopedic Hospital. The doctor complained of fatigue. My parents rushed into the room, looking very old and very pale. That's when reality caught up with me. Numb and in shock, I began to cry.

The doctor worked efficiently, snapping my dislocated toes back into place and sewing up my right foot. Later, in the oper-ating room, his scalpel sliced a long red line deep into my flesh, cutting through the muscles that had worked for me so well. He removed bone from my pelvis and grafted it to the forty-odd fragments of my right thighbone. Finally, he hammered a narrow metal rod down the center of my bone from the hip, a kind of internal cast.

I was semiconscious for three days, in a drugged sleep that barely separated me from the agonizing, unrelenting pain. Sometime in the evening of the third day I awoke in darkness when I sensed someone quiet as a shadow, sitting nearby.

Joy got up and knelt by my bedside, stroking my forehead as I turned away in shame. She whispered to me, "I came as soon as I heard." I wished her to share my victories; she always saw me in defeat. I bit my lip and tasted tears. Joy gently turned my face to hers and looked into my eyes. "Socrates has a message for you, Danny; he asked me to tell you this story:"

I closed my eyes and listened intently.

An old man and his son worked a small farm, with only one horse to pull the plow. One day, the horse ran away.

"How terrible," sympathized the neighbors. "What bad luck."

"Who knows whether it is bad luck or good luck," the farmer replied.

A week later, the horse returned from the mountains, leading five wild mares into the barn.

"What wonderful luck!" said the neighbors.

"Good luck? Bad luck? Who knows?" answered the old man.

The next day, the son, trying to tame one of the horses, fell and broke his leg.

"How terrible. What bad luck!"

"Bad luck? Good luck?"

The army came to all the farms to take the young men for war, but the farmer's son was of no use to them, so he was spared.

"Good? Bad?"

I smiled sadly, then bit my lip as I was assaulted by another wave of pain.

Joy soothed me with her voice. "Everything has a purpose, Danny; it's for you to make the best use of it."

"How will I ever make use of this accident?"

"There are no accidents, Danny. Everything is a lesson. Trust your life. Everything has a purpose, a purpose, a *purpose*," she repeated, whispering in my ear.

"But my gymnastics, my training..."

"*This* is your training. Let the pain purify your mind and body. It will burn through many obstructions." She saw the questioning look in my eyes, and added, "A warrior doesn't seek pain, but if pain comes, he uses it. Now rest, Danny, rest." She slipped out behind the entering nurse.

"Don't go, Joy," I muttered and fell into a deep sleep, remembering nothing more.

Friends visited and my parents came every day; but for most of twenty-one endless days I lay alone, flat on my back. I watched the white ceiling and meditated for hours, battered by thoughts of melancholy, self-pity, and futile hope.

On a Tuesday morning, leaning on new crutches, I stepped out into the bright September sunlight and hobbled to my parents' car. I'd lost almost thirty pounds — my pants hung loosely on protruding hipbones and my right leg looked like a stick with a long purple scar down the side.

A fresh breeze caressed my face on this rare, smogless day. The wind carried flowered scents I'd forgotten; the chirping of birds in a nearby tree mixed with the sound of traffic created a symphony for my newly awakened senses. I stayed with my parents for a few days, resting in the hot sun and swimming slowly through the shallow end of the pool, painfully forcing my sutured leg muscles to work. I ate sparingly — yogurt, nuts, cheese, and fresh vegetables. I was beginning to regain my vitality.

Friends invited me to stay with them for a few weeks at their home in Santa Monica, five blocks from the beach. I accepted, welcoming the chance to spend more time in the open air.

Each morning I walked slowly to the warm sand, and, laying my crutches down, sat by the waves. I listened to the gulls and the surf, then closed my eyes and meditated for hours, oblivious to the world around me. Berkeley, Socrates, and my past seemed far away, in another dimension, another life.

Soon I began a program of exercise, slowly at first, then more intensely, until I was spending hours each day sweating in the hot sun, doing push-ups, sit-ups, chin-ups. I carefully pressed up to handstands, then pumped up and down, again and again, puffing with exertion until every muscle had worked to its limit and my body glistened. Then I would hop on one leg into the shallow surf and sit dreaming of lofty somersaults until the salt water washed my sweat and soaring dreams into the sea.

I trained fiercely until my muscles were as hard and defined as a marble statue. I became one of the beach regulars who made the sea and sand their way of life. Malcolm the masseur would sit down on my blanket and tell jokes; Doc, the Rand Corporation think-tank whiz, would drop by my blanket every day and talk with me about politics and women, mostly women.

I had time to consider all that had happened to me since I'd met Socrates. I thought about life and its purpose, death and its mystery. And I thought about my mysterious teacher — his words, his animated expressions. Mostly though, I remembered his laughter.

The warmth of the October sun faded into November clouds. Fewer people came to the beach, and during this time of solitude, I enjoyed a peace I'd not felt for many years. I imagined staying on that beach the rest of my life, but knew I'd be going back to school after Christmas.

My doctor gave me the results of my X-rays. "Your leg is healing well, Mr. Millman — unusually well, I should say. But I caution you; don't get your hopes up. The nature of your accident doesn't make it likely that you'll be able to do gymnastics again." I said nothing.

Soon I said my farewells to my parents and boarded a flight back to Berkeley.

Rick picked me up at the airport; I stayed with him and Sid for a few days until I found a studio apartment near campus.

I created a daily routine until classes started: Each morning, gripping my crutches, I'd make my way to the gym, train on the weight machines, and fall exhausted into the swimming pool, where, assisted by the water's buoyancy, I'd force my leg to the point of pain, trying to walk — always, always to the point of pain.

Afterward, I would lie on the pool deck, stretching my muscles to retain the suppleness I'd need for future training. Finally, I rested, reading in the library until I fell into a light sleep.

I had called Socrates to tell him I was back. He wasn't much for talking on the phone and told me to visit him when I could walk without crutches. That was OK with me; I wasn't ready to see him yet.

It was a lonely Christmas that year until Pat and Dennis, two of my teammates, knocked on my apartment door, grabbed me, and practically carried me down to the car. We drove toward Reno, up into the snow, and stopped at Donner Summit. While Pat and Dennis ran through the snow, wrestling, throwing snowballs, and sledding down the hill, I hobbled carefully through the frozen field and sat on a log.

My thoughts floated back to the coming semester, and to the gymnastics room. I wondered if my leg would ever heal straight and strong. Snow dropped from a branch, thudding with a slushy sound to the frozen ground, waking me from my reverie.

On the way home, Pat and Dennis were singing bawdy songs; I watched white crystals float down around us, glittering in our car's lights as the sun began to set. I thought about my derailed future and wished that I could leave my whirling mind behind me, buried in a white grave beside the road in the snowy mountains.

Just after the holidays I made a brief visit to L.A. to see my doctor, who let me trade in my crutches for a shiny black cane. Then I headed back to school — and to Socrates.

It was Wednesday night at 11:40 P.M. when I limped through the doorway of the office and saw his radiant face. And I knew I was home again. I'd almost forgotten what it was like to sit and sip tea with my old mentor in the quiet of the night. It was a more subtle, and in many ways greater, pleasure than all my athletic victories. I looked at this man who had become my teacher and saw things I'd never seen before.

In the past I had noticed a light that seemed to encircle him, but I'd assumed it was only my tired eyes. I wasn't tired now, and there was no doubt about it — it was a barely perceptible aura. "Socrates," I said, "there's a light shining around your body. Where does it come from?"

"Clean living," he grinned. Then the bell clanged and he went out to make someone else laugh, under the pretext of servicing a car. Socrates dispensed more than gasoline. Maybe it was that aura, that energy or emotion. Anyway, people nearly always left happier than when they had arrived.

It wasn't the glowing, however, that impressed me most about him; it was his simplicity, his economy of motion and of action. I hadn't truly appreciated any of this before. It was as if I saw more deeply into Socrates with every new lesson I learned. As I came to see the complexities of my mind, I realized how he had already transcended his.

When he returned to the office I asked, "Socrates, where is Joy now? Will I see her again soon?"

He smiled as if glad to hear my questions again. "Dan, I don't know where she is; that girl is a mystery to me — always was."

I then told him about the accident and its aftermath. He listened quietly and intently, nodding his head.

"Dan, you're no longer the young fool who walked into this office over a year ago."

"Has it been a year? It seems like ten," I joked. "Are you saying I'm no longer a fool?"

"No, only that you're no longer young."

"Hey, that's real heartwarming, Soc."

"Now you're a fool with spirit, Dan. And that's a very big difference. You still have a chance of finding the gate."

"Gate?"

"The realm of the warrior is guarded by something like a gate. It is well hidden, like a monastery in the mountains. Many knock, but few enter."

"Well, show me where it is. I'll find a way in."

"It's not so simple, bumpkin. The gate exists inside you, and you alone must find it. But you're not ready yet, not nearly ready. If you attempted to pass through the gate now, it would mean almost certain death. There's much to be done before you're prepared to pass through."

When Socrates talked, it sounded like a pronouncement. "Dan, we've talked much; you've seen visions and learned lessons. Now it's time you became fully responsible for your own behavior. To find the gate, you'll have to follow — "

"The House Rules?" I interrupted.

He laughed, then the bell clanged as a car rolled smoothly through a rain puddle into the station. I watched through the misty window as Socrates walked quickly out into the drizzle, wearing his poncho. I could see him put the gas nozzle in, go around to the driver's side, and say something to a bearded, blond-haired man in the car.

The window misted over again, so I wiped it clean with my sleeve in time to see them laughing. Then Socrates opened the door to the office, and a draft of cold air slapped me harshly, bringing with it my first awareness that I didn't feel well at all.

Still, when Socrates started to make some tea, I said, "Please, sit down, Soc. I'll make the tea." He sat, nodding his head in approval. I leaned against the desk for a moment, feeling dizzy. My throat was sore; maybe the tea would help.

As I filled the kettle and placed it on the hot plate, I asked, "Do I have to blaze some kind of inner path to this gate, then?"

"Yes, everyone must. You pave the way with your own work." Anticipating my next question, he said, "Each of us has the capacity to find the gate and pass through, but few are interested. This is very important. I didn't decide to teach you because of any unique capacity you possessed — as a matter of fact, you have glaring weaknesses along with your strong points — but you have the *will* to make this journey."

That struck a resonant chord. "I guess you could compare it to gymnastics, Soc. Even someone who is overweight, weak, or inflexible can become a fine gymnast, but the preparation is longer and more difficult."

"Yes, that's exactly what it's like. And I can tell you this: your path is going to be steep and rocky."

My head felt feverish, and I ached all over. I leaned against the desk again. Out of the corner of my eye I saw Socrates come toward me, reaching out for my head. Oh no, not now; I'm not up to it, I thought. But he was only feeling my clammy forehead. Then he checked the glands in my neck, looked at my face and eyes, and felt my pulse.

"Dan, your energies are way out of balance, and your spleen is probably swollen. I suggest you visit a physician. Tonight. Now."

I was feeling really miserable by the time I limped to Cowell Hospital. My throat was burning, my body aching. The doctor confirmed Soc's diagnosis. My spleen was badly swollen due to a severe case of mononucleosis. I was admitted to the infirmary.

During that first fitful, feverish night, I dreamed that I had one huge leg and one shriveled one. When I tried to swing on the bars or tumble, everything was crooked; then I fell and fell and fell into the late afternoon of the next day, when Socrates walked in with a bouquet of dried flowers.

"Socrates," I said weakly, delighted by his unexpected visit, "you shouldn't have."

"Yes, I should have," he replied.

"I'll have the nurse put them in a vase; I'll think of you whenever I look at them," I grinned weakly.

"They're not to look at — they're to eat," he said, leaving the room. A few minutes later, he returned with a glass of hot water. Crushing some of the flowers, he wrapped them in a piece of cheesecloth he'd brought and dipped the tea bag into the water. "This tea will strengthen you and help cleanse the blood. Here, drink." It tasted bitter — strong medicine.

Then he took a small bottle of yellow liquid in which were floating more crushed herbs, and massaged the liquid deep into my right leg, directly over the scar. I wondered what the nurse, a very pretty, businesslike young woman, would say if she came in.

"What is that yellow stuff in the bottle, Soc?"

"Urine, with a few herbs."

"Urine!" I said, pulling my leg away from him in disgust.

"Don't be silly," he said, grabbing my leg and pulling it back. "Urine is a respected elixir in the ancient healing traditions."

I closed my tired, aching eyes; my head was throbbing like jungle drums. I felt the fever starting to rise again. Socrates put his hand against my head, then felt the pulse in my wrist. "Good, the herbs are taking effect. Tonight should be the crisis; tomorrow, you'll feel better."

I managed a barely audible, "Thank you, Doc Soc."

He reached over and put his hand on my solar plexus. Almost immediately, everything in my body intensified. I thought my head would explode. The fever started to burn me up; my glands pulsated. Worst of all was a terrible burning pain in my right leg at the site of the injury.

"Stop it, Socrates — stop!" I yelled.

He took his hand away and I collapsed into the bed. "I've

just introduced a little more energy into your body than you're used to; it will accelerate the healing processes. It burns only where you have knots. If you were free of obstructions — if your mind was clear, your heart open, and your body free of tension — you'd experience the energy as an indescribable pleasure, better than sex. You'd think you were in heaven, and in a way, you'd be right."

"Sometimes you scare me, Socrates."

"Warriors are always held in fear and awe." He grinned. "You also look like a warrior: slim, supple, and strong from your rudimentary preparation in gymnastics. But you have a lot of work to do before you earn the kind of vitality *I* enjoy."

I was too weak to argue.

The nurse walked in. "Time to take your temperature, Mr. Millman." Socrates had risen politely when she entered. I lay in bed looking pale and miserable. The contrast between the two of us had never felt greater than at that moment. The nurse smiled at Socrates, who grinned back. "I think your son is going to be just fine with a little rest," she said.

"Just what I was telling him," Soc said, his eyes twinkling. She smiled at him again — was that a flirtatious look she gave him? With a rustle of white, she glided out the door.

Socrates sighed. "Ah, there's something about a woman in uniform." Then he put his hand on my forehead. I fell into a deep sleep.

The next morning, I felt like a new man. The doctor's eyebrows rose as he checked my spleen, felt for my swollen glands, and rechecked my chart. He was dumbfounded. "I can't find anything wrong with you, Mr. Millman." He sounded almost apologetic. "You can go home after lunch. Get plenty of rest." He walked out, staring at my chart.

The nurse rustled by again. "Help!" I yelled.

"What is it?" she said, stepping quickly inside.

"I can't understand it, nurse. I think I'm having heart trouble. Every time you go by, my pulse gets erotic."

"Don't you mean erratic?" she said.

"Whatever."

She smiled. "It sounds like you're ready to go home."

"That's what everyone keeps telling me, but I'm sure I'll need private nursing care."

She winked, turned, and walked away. "Nurse! Don't leave me," I cried.

That afternoon, walking home, I was astonished by the improvement in my leg. I still limped badly, throwing my hip out to the side whenever I took a step, but I could almost walk without my cane. Maybe there was something to Soc's urine treatment or the battery-charge he had given me.

School had begun. I was again surrounded by other students and books and assignments, but that was all secondary to me now. I played the game without concern. I had more important things to do in a small gas station on the corner of Oxford and Hearst.

After a long nap, I walked to the station. The moment I sat down, Soc said, "We have work to do."

"What?" I said, stretching and yawning.

"A complete overhaul."

"Oh, a big job?"

"You bet; we're going to overhaul you."

"Oh, yeah?" I said. Oh hell, I thought.

"Like the phoenix, you're going to throw yourself into the flames and rise from your ashes."

"A metaphor, I hope."

Socrates was just getting started. "Right now you're a tangled mass of twisted circuits and outmoded programs. We're going to rewire old habits of acting, of thinking, of dreaming, and of seeing the world. Most of what you *are* is a series of bad habits."

He was starting to get to me. "Damn it, Socrates, I've overcome some difficult hurdles, and I'm doing the best I can. Can't you show me some respect?"

Socrates threw his head back and laughed. He walked over and pulled my shirt out. As I was tucking it back in, he mussed up my hair. "Listen up, O Great Buffoon, everyone wants respect. But it is not just a matter of saying, 'Please respect me.' You must earn respect by acting respectable — and the respect of a warrior is not easily earned."

I counted to ten, took a deep breath, and asked, "How, then, am I going to earn your respect, O Great and Awesome Warrior?"

"By changing your act."

"What act is that?"

"Your 'poor me' act, of course. Stop being so proud of mediocrity; show some spirit!" Grinning, Socrates jumped up and slapped me playfully on my cheek, then poked me in the ribs.

"Cut it out!" I yelled, in no mood for his play. I reached out to grab his arm, but he leaped lightly up on his desk. Then he leaped over my head, spun, and pushed me backward onto the couch. Climbing angrily to my feet I tried to push him back, but just as I touched him he leaped *backward* over the desk. And I fell forward onto the carpet. "Goddamn it!" I raged, seeing red. He slipped out the door into the garage. I limped after him in pursuit.

Socrates perched on a fender and scratched his head. "Why, Dan, you're angry."

"Stunning observation," I fumed, panting heavily.

"Good," he said. "Considering your predicament, you *should* be angry. Nothing wrong with anger or any other emotion. Just pay attention to how you behave." Soc deftly began to change the spark plugs on a VW. "Anger is a powerful tool to transform old habits" — he removed an old plug with the sparkplug wrench — "and replace them with new ones." He threaded a new plug into the block, tightening it with a light tug of the wrench. "Fear and sorrow inhibit action; anger generates it. When you learn to make proper use of your anger, you can change fear and sorrow to anger, then turn anger to action. That's the body's secret of internal alchemy."

Back in the office, Socrates drew some water from the springwater dispenser and put on the evening's tea specialty, rose hips, as he continued. "To rid yourself of old patterns, focus all your energy not on struggling with the old, but on building the new."

"How can I control my habits if I can't even seem to control my emotions?"

"You don't need to control emotion," he said. "Emotions are natural, like passing weather. Sometimes it's fear, sometimes sorrow or anger. Emotions are not the problem. The key is to transform the energy of emotion into constructive action."

I got up, took the whistling kettle off the hot plate, and poured the steaming water into our mugs. "Can you give me a specific example, Socrates?"

"Spend time with a baby."

Smiling, I blew on my tea. "Funny, I never thought of babies as masters of emotions."

"When a baby is upset, it expresses itself in banshee wails — pure crying. It doesn't wonder about whether it *should* be crying. Babies accept their emotions completely. They let feelings flow, then let them go. In this way, infants are fine teachers. Learn their lessons and you'll dissolve old habits."

A Ford Ranchero wagon pulled into the station. Socrates went around to the driver's seat while I, chuckling, grabbed the gas hose and removed the gas cap. Inspired by his revelations, I yelled over the roof of the car, "Soc, I'm ready to tear those old habits to shreds!" Then I glanced down at the passengers — three shocked nuns. I choked on my words, turned beet red, and busied myself with washing the windows. Socrates leaned against the pump and buried his face in his hands.

After the Ranchero pulled out, much to my relief, another customer drove in. It was the blond man again — the one with the curly beard. He jumped out of the car and gave Socrates a bear hug. "Good to see you, Joseph," Socrates said.

"Same here…uh, *Socrates*, isn't it?" He turned to me and grinned.

"Joseph, this young question machine is named Dan. Push a button and he asks a question. Highly amusing, really."

Joseph shook my hand. "Has the old man mellowed in his declining years?" he asked with a broad smile.

Before I could assure him that Soc was probably more ornery than ever, the 'old man' interrupted. "Oh, I've really gotten lazy. Dan has it much easier than you did."

"Oh, I see," Joseph said, maintaining a serious countenance. "You haven't taken the boy on any 100-mile runs or worked with the burning coals yet, hmm?"

"No, nothing like that. We're just about to start with the basics, like how to eat, walk, and breathe."

Joseph's laugh was so merry, I found myself laughing with him. "Speaking of eating," he said, "Why don't both of you come to the café this morning. You'll be my private guests, and I'll whip up something for breakfast."

I was just about to decline — I had a class — when Socrates said, "We'd be delighted. The morning shift gets on in half an hour — we'll walk over."

"Great. See you then." He paid Soc for the gas and drove off.

"Is Joseph a warrior, like you, Soc?"

"No one is a warrior like me," he answered, laughing. "Nor would anyone want to be. Each of us has natural qualities. For example, while you've excelled in gymnastics, Joseph has mastered the preparation of food."

"Oh, you mean cooking?"

"Not exactly. Joseph specializes in uncooked food. Fresh, natural, enzymes, and all that. You'll soon taste for yourself. After Joseph's culinary magic, you'll have little tolerance for fast-food joints."

"What's so special about his food?"

"Only two things, really — both subtle. First, he gives his complete attention to what he does; second, love is one of the primary ingredients in everything he makes. It has a sweet after-taste."

Soc's replacement, a lanky teenager, came in with his usual grunted greeting. We left, crossed the street, and headed south. My limping pace quickened to keep up with Soc's strides as we took the scenic route down side streets, avoiding early morning rush-hour traffic.

Crunching over dried leaves, we walked past the varied array of dwellings that characterize Berkeley's housing, a mixture of Victorian, Spanish Colonial, neo-alpine funk, and box-like apartment houses catering to many of the 30,000 students.

As we walked, we talked. Socrates began. "You're going to

need unusual energy to cut through the mists of your mind and find your way to the gate. So purifying, regenerative practices are essential."

"Could you run that by me again?"

"Sure. We're going to clean you out, take you apart, and put you back together again."

"Oh, why didn't you say that in the first place," I teased.

"You'll need to refine every human function — moving, sleeping, breathing, thinking, feeling — and eating. Of all the human activities, eating is one of the most important to stabilize first."

"Wait a minute, Socrates. Eating isn't really a problem area for me. I'm slim, I generally feel pretty good, and my gymnastics proves I have plenty of energy. How is changing a few things in my diet going to make a difference?"

"Your present diet," he said, glancing up through the sunlit branches of a beautiful tree, "may give you 'plenty' of energy, but it also makes you groggy, affects your moods, and lowers your level of awareness."

"How can changing my diet affect my energy?" I argued. "I mean, I take in calories, and they represent a certain amount of energy."

"True, as far as it goes, but a warrior must recognize more subtle influences. Our primary source of energy is the sun. But in general, the human being — that's you — "

"Thanks for the concession."

"In your present state of evolution, you cannot 'eat sunlight' except in limited ways. When humanity does develop this ability, the digestive organs will become vestigial and laxative companies will go out of business. For now, a proper diet allows you to make the most direct use of the sun's energy. This energy helps you focus your attention, sharpening your concentration into a slashing blade."

"Just by cutting donuts from my diet?"

"And a few other odds and ends."

"One of the Japanese Olympic gymnasts once told me that it's not your bad habits that count, but your good ones."

"That means your good habits must become so strong that

they dissolve those which are not useful." Socrates pointed ahead to a small café on Shattuck near Ashby. I'd walked past many times without really noticing it.

"So, you believe in natural foods?" I said as we crossed the street.

"It's not a matter of believing but of doing. I can tell you this: I eat only what is wholesome, and I eat only as much as I need. In order to appreciate what you call 'natural' foods, you have to sharpen your instincts; you have to become a natural man."

"Sounds ascetic to me. Don't you even have a little ice cream now and then?"

"My diet may at first seem spartan compared to the indulgences you call 'moderation,' Dan, but I take great pleasure in what I eat because I've developed the capacity to enjoy the simplest foods. And so will you."

We knocked on the door. "Come in, come in," Joseph said enthusiastically, welcoming us to his tiny café. It looked more like a home: Thick carpets covered the floor. Heavy, polished, rough-hewn tables were placed around the room, and the soft straight-backed chairs looked like antiques. Tapestries covered the walls, except for one wall almost completely hidden by a huge aquarium of colorful fish. Morning light poured through a skylight overhead. We sat directly below it, in the warm rays of the sun, occasionally shaded by clouds drifting overhead.

Joseph approached us, carrying two plates over his head. With a flourish, he placed them in front of us, serving Socrates first, then me. "Looks delicious!" said Socrates, tucking his napkin into the neck of his shirt. I looked down. There before me, on a white plate, were a sliced carrot and a piece of lettuce. I stared at it in consternation.

At my expression, Socrates almost fell out of his chair laughing and Joseph had to lean against a table. "Ah," I said, with a sigh of relief. "A joke, then."

Without another word, Joseph took the plates and returned with two beautiful wooden bowls. In each bowl was a perfectly carved, miniature replica of a mountain. The mountain itself was a blended combination of cantaloupe and honeydew melon. Small chunks of walnuts and almonds, individually carved, became brown boulders. The craggy cliffs were made from apples and thin slices of cheese. The trees were made of many pieces of parsley, each pruned to a perfect shape, like bonsai trees. An icing of yogurt capped the peak. Around the base were halved grapes and a ring of fresh strawberries.

I sat and stared. "Joseph, it's too beautiful. I can't eat this; I want to take a picture of it." Socrates, I noticed, had already begun eating, nibbling slowly, as was his manner. So I attacked the mountain in my customary fashion and was almost done, when Socrates suddenly started gobbling his food. I realized he was mimicking me.

I did my best to take small bites, breathing deeply between each bite as he did, but it seemed frustratingly slow.

"The pleasure from eating, Dan, is more than the taste of the food and the feeling of a full belly. Learn to enjoy the entire process — the hunger beforehand, the careful preparation, setting an attractive table, chewing, breathing, smelling, tasting, swallowing, and the feeling of lightness and energy after the meal. You can even enjoy the full and easy elimination of the food after it's digested. When you pay attention to all elements of the process, you'll begin to appreciate simple meals."

"The irony of your present eating habits is that while you fear missing a meal, you aren't fully aware of the meals you do eat."

"I'm not afraid of missing a meal."

"Glad to hear that. It will make the coming week easier for you."

"Huh?"

"This is your last meal for the next seven days." Soc proceeded to outline a purifying fast that I was to begin immediately. Diluted fruit juice and plain herb teas were to be my only fare.

"Hold on, Socrates. I need protein and iron to help my leg heal; I need my energy for gymnastics." It was no use. Socrates could be a very unreasonable man.

We helped Joseph with a few chores, talked for a while, thanked him, and left. I was already hungry. While we walked back toward campus, Socrates summarized the disciplines I was to follow until my body regained its natural instincts. "In a few years, there will be no need for rules. You can experiment and trust your instincts. For now, however, you're to avoid foods that contain refined sugar, refined flour, and meat, as well as coffee, alcohol, tobacco, or any other drugs. Focus on fresh fruits, vegetables, whole grains, and legumes. I don't believe in extremes, but for now, make breakfast a fresh fruit meal, with occasional yogurt. Your lunch, your main meal, should be a raw salad, baked or steamed potato, and whole-grain bread or cooked grains. Dinner should be a raw salad and, on occasion, lightly steamed vegetables. Make good use of raw, unsalted seeds and nuts at every meal."

"I guess by now you're quite an expert on nuts, Soc," I grumbled.

On the way home, we passed by a neighborhood grocery store. I was about to go inside and get some cookies when I remembered that I was no longer allowed to eat store-bought cookies. And for the next six days and twenty-three hours, I wouldn't be eating anything at all.

"Socrates, I'm hungry."

"I never said that the training of a warrior would be a piece of cake."

We walked through the campus just between classes, so Sproul Plaza was filled with people. I gazed wistfully at the pretty coeds. Socrates touched my arm. "That reminds me, Dan. Cookies aren't the only sweet things you're going to have to avoid for a while."

I stopped dead in my tracks. "I want to make sure I understand you. Can you be more specific?"

"Sure. Until you're sufficiently mature, keep it in your pants."

"But, Socrates," I argued, as if on trial for my life, "that's puritanical, unreasonable, and unhealthy. Cutting down on food is one thing, but this is different!" I started quoting the "Playboy Philosophy," Albert Ellis, Robert Rimmer, Jacqueline Susann, and the Marquis de Sade. I even threw in Reader's Digest and "Dear Abby," but nothing moved him.

He said, "There's no point in my trying to explain my reasons; you're just going to have to find your future thrills in fresh air, fresh food, fresh water, fresh awareness, and sunshine."

"How can I possibly do all that?"

"Consider the final words the Buddha spoke to his disciples."

"What's that?" I asked awaiting inspiration.

"'Just do your best.'" With that, he vanished into the crowd.

The next week, my rites of initiation got under way. While my stomach growled, Soc filled my nights with "basic" exercises, teaching me how to breathe more deeply and slowly. I plodded on, doing my best, feeling lethargic, looking forward to my (ugh!) diluted fruit juice and herb tea, dreaming about steaks and sweet rolls. And I didn't even particularly *like* steaks or sweet rolls!

He told me to breathe with my belly one day, and to breathe with my heart the next. He began to criticize my walking, my talking, the way my eyes wandered around the room as my "mind wandered around the universe." Nothing I did seemed to satisfy him.

Over and over he corrected me, sometimes gently, sometimes harshly. "Proper posture is a way of blending with gravity, Dan. Proper attitude is a way of blending with life." And so it went.

The third day of the fast was the hardest. I was weak and cranky; I had headaches and bad breath. "All part of the purification process, Dan. Your body is cleansing itself," he told me. At workout, all I did was lie around and stretch.

By the seventh day, I was actually feeling good. My hunger had disappeared; in its stead was a pleasant lassitude and a feeling of lightness. Workouts actually improved. Limited only by my weak leg, I trained hard, feeling relaxed and more supple than ever.

When I started eating on the eighth day, beginning with very small amounts of fruit, I had to use all my willpower not to start gorging myself on whatever food remained on Soc's menu for me.

He tolerated no complaints, no back talk. In fact, he didn't want me to talk *at all* unless it was absolutely necessary. "No more idle jabbering," he said. "What comes out of your mouth is as important as what goes into it." I learned to censor most of my more inane comments. It actually felt good to talk less, once I started getting the knack of it. I felt calmer, somehow. But after a few weeks I longed for more conversation.

"Soc, I'll bet you a dollar that I can make you say more than two words."

He held out his hand, palm up, saying, "You lose."

Because of my gymnastics successes in the past, I believed my training with Socrates would go the same way. But before long I realized that, as Socrates had predicted, it wasn't going to be a piece of cake.

My main problem was fitting in socially with my friends. Rick, Sid, and I took dates to LaVal's for pizza. Everyone else, including my date, shared an extra-large sausage pizza; I ordered a small whole-wheat, vegetarian special. They had milk shakes or beer; I sipped my apple juice. They wanted to go to Fenton's Ice Cream Parlor afterward. While they ate their sundaes, I ordered mineral water and ended up sucking on a piece of ice. I looked at them enviously; they looked back at me as if I were a little crazy. And maybe they were right. Anyway, my social life was collapsing under the weight of my disciplines.

I would walk blocks out of my way to avoid the donut shops, food stands, and outdoor restaurants near campus. My cravings and compulsions only seemed to grow stronger, but I fought back. If I turned into a jellyfish over a jelly donut, how could I face Socrates?

Over time, though, I began to feel a growing resistance. I complained to Socrates, in spite of his dark look. "Soc, you're no fun anymore. You've become an ordinary grumpy old man; you never even glow."

He glowered at me. "No more magic tricks," was all he said. That was just it — no tricks, no sex, no potato chips, no hamburgers, no candy, no donuts, no fun, and no rest; only discipline inside and out.

January trudged by; February had flown, and now March was nearly over. The team was finishing the season without me.

Again I told Socrates my feelings, but he offered no consolation, no support. "Socrates, I'm a real spiritual boy scout. My friends don't want to go out with me anymore. You're ruining my life!"

He only resumed his paperwork and said, "Just do your best."

"Well, thank you for the stirring pep talk." I was starting to resent having another person — even Socrates — direct my life.

Still, I fulfilled every rule with teeth-clenching determination until one day, during workout, in walked the dazzling nurse who had starred in my erotic fantasies since my stay in the hospital. She sat down quietly and watched our aerial routines. Almost immediately, I noticed, everyone in the gym was inspired to a new level of energy, and I was no exception.

Pretending to be immersed in practice, I glanced at her every now and then out of the corner of my eye. Her tight silk pants and halter top had snared my concentration; my mind kept drifting off to more exotic forms of gymnastics. For the rest of workout I was acutely conscious of her attention.

She disappeared just before the end of training. I showered, dressed, and headed up the stairs. She was waiting at the top of the staircase, leaning seductively against the banister. I don't even remember walking up the final flight of stairs.

"Hi, Dan Millman. I'm Valerie. You look much better than when I cared for you in the hospital."

"I am much better, Nurse Valerie." I grinned. "And I'm so glad you cared." She laughed and stretched invitingly.

"Dan, would you walk me home? It's getting dark out, and a strange man has been following me."

I was about to point out that it was early April and the sun wouldn't be going down for another hour, but then thought, "What the hell — a petty detail."

We walked, we talked, and we ended up having dinner at her apartment. She opened her bottle of "special wine for special occasions." I merely had a sip, but it was the beginning of the end. I was sizzling, hotter than the steak on the grill. There was a moment when a little voice asked, "Are you a man or a jellyfish?" Another little voice answered, "I'm one horny jellyfish." That night I washed out on every discipline I'd been given. I ate whatever she gave me. I started with a cup of clam chowder, then salad and steak. And for dessert, I had several helpings of Valerie.

For the next three days I didn't sleep very well, preoccupied with how to present my true confession to Socrates.

Prepared for the worst, I walked into the office and told him everything. Then I held my breath. Socrates didn't speak for a long time. Finally he said, "I notice you haven't learned to breathe yet." Before I could reply, he held up his hand. "Dan, *I* can understand how you might choose an ice-cream cone or a fling with a pretty woman over your training, but can *you* understand it?" He paused. "There is no praise, no blame. You now understand the compelling hungers in your belly and your loins. That is good. But consider this: I've asked you to do your best. Was that really your best?"

Socrates turned his eyes on "bright"; they shined through me. "Come back in a month, but only if you've strictly applied the disciplines. See the young woman if you wish, but no matter what urges you may feel, reclaim your will."

"I'll do it, Socrates; I swear I will! I really understand now."

"Neither resolutions nor understanding will ever make you strong. Resolutions have sincerity, logic has clarity; but neither has the energy you will need. Let anger strengthen your resolve. See you next month."

I knew that if I forgot the disciplines again, it would be the end. With new determination, I promised myself, no seductive woman, donut, or piece of roasted cow flesh is going to benumb my will again. I'll master my impulses or die.

Valerie called me the next day. I felt all the familiar stirrings at the sound of her voice, which had moaned in my ear not long before. "Danny, I'd love to see you tonight. Are you free? Oh, good. I get off work at seven. Shall I meet you at the gym? OK, see you then — bye."

I took her to Joseph's café that night for a supreme salad surprise. I noticed that Valerie was flirting with Joseph. And with every other nice-looking male who was nearby and breathing.

Later, we returned to her apartment. We sat and talked a while. She offered wine; I asked for juice. She touched my hair and kissed me softly, murmuring in my ear. I kissed her back with feeling. Then my inner voice came through loud and clear: Get out while you can, Bozo.

I sat up, taking a deep breath. I stumbled through the lamest, most idiotic explanation imaginable. "Valerie, you know I find you attractive, but I'm involved in some, uh, personal disciplines that no longer allow — well...I enjoy your company and all, but...From now on, please think of me as an intimate friend, or a brother, or a loving p-p-priest." I almost couldn't get it out.

She took a deep breath, smoothed out her hair, and said, "Dan, it's really good to be with someone who isn't interested only in sex."

"Well," I said, encouraged. "I'm glad to hear you feel that way, because I know we can have other kinds of fun, and..."

She looked at her watch. "Oh, will you look at the time — and I have to work early tomorrow, too — so I'll say good night, Dan. Thank you for dinner. It was lovely."

I called her the next day, but her phone was busy. I left a message, but she didn't return it. I saw her a week later after practice; she was hand in hand with Scott, one of the guys on the team. They walked right by me as I came up the stairs — so close that I could smell her perfume. She nodded politely. Scott leered back and gave me a meaningful wink. I didn't know a wink could hurt that much.

With a desperate hunger that a raw salad repast couldn't possibly satisfy, I found myself in front of the Charbroiler. I smelled the sizzling hamburgers, basted with special sauce. I remembered all the good times I'd had, eating burgers with lettuce and tomatoes — and friends. In a daze, I went in without thinking, walked right up to the woman behind the counter, and heard myself say, "One charbroiled with double cheese, please."

116

She gave it to me and I sat down, gazed at the burger, and took a huge bite. Suddenly I realized what I was doing — choosing between Socrates and a cheeseburger. I spit it out, threw it angrily in the trash, and walked out. It was over; I was through being a slave to random impulses.

That night marked the beginning of a new glow of self-respect and a feeling of personal power. I knew it would get easier now.

Small changes began to add up in my life. Ever since I was a kid, I'd suffered all kinds of minor symptoms, like a runny nose at night when the air cooled, headaches, stomach upsets, and mood swings, all of which I thought were normal and inevitable. Now they had all vanished.

I felt a constant sense of lightness and energy that radiated around me. Maybe that accounted for the number of women flirting with me, the little kids and dogs coming up to me and wanting to play. A few of my teammates started asking for advice about personal problems. No longer a small boat in a stormy sea, I started to feel like the Rock of Gibraltar.

I told Socrates about these experiences. He nodded. "Your energy level is rising. People, animals, and even things are attracted to energy fields. That's how it works."

"House Rules?" I asked.

"House Rules." Then he added, "But it may be premature for self-congratulation. Keep a sense of perspective. You've only graduated from kindergarten."

School ended for the year almost without my noticing it. Exams went smoothly; the studies that had always seemed to be a major struggle for me had become a minor piece of business to get out of the way. The team left for a short vacation, then returned for summer workouts. I was beginning to walk without my cane and even tried to run very slowly a few times a week. I continued pushing myself with all the discipline and endurance I could find inside. And I did my best to pay attention to eating, moving, and breathing — but my best was still not very good.

Socrates only increased his demands. "Now that your energy is building, you can begin training in earnest."

I practiced breathing so slowly that it took one minute to complete each breath. When combined with intense concentration and control of specific muscle groups, this breathing exercise heated my body up like a sauna and allowed me to remain comfortable outside no matter what the temperature.

I was excited to realize that I was developing the same power that Socrates had shown me the night we met. For the first time, I began to believe that maybe, just maybe, I could become a peaceful warrior like him. Instead of feeling left out, I now felt superior to my friends. When a friend complained of illness or other problems that I knew could be remedied by simply eating properly, I offered what advice I could.

I took my newfound confidence with me to the station one night, feeling sure that I was about to learn some ancient and esoteric secrets of India, Tibet, or China. But as soon as I stepped through the door, Socrates handed me a scrub brush and said, "Make those toilets shine." For weeks afterward, I did so many menial tasks around the station that I had no time for my real training. I lifted tires for an hour, then took out the trash. I swept the garage and straightened the tools. Life with Socrates was now filled with drudgery and boredom.

At the same time, it was impossibly demanding. He'd give me five minutes to do a half-hour job, then criticize me mercilessly if it wasn't done thoroughly. He was unfair, unreasonable, and even insulting. As I was considering my disgust with this state of affairs, Socrates stepped into the garage. "You left dirt on the bathroom floor."

"Someone must have used the bathroom after I finished," I said.

"No excuses," he said, and added, "Throw out the garbage."

I was so mad that I gripped my broom handle like a sword. "But I just threw the garbage out *five minutes ago,* Socrates. Do you remember, or are you getting senile?"

He grinned. "I'm talking about this garbage, baboon!" He tapped his head and winked at me. The broom clattered to the floor.

Another evening when I was sweeping the garage, Socrates called me into the office. I sat down, sullen, awaiting orders. "Dan, you still haven't learned to breathe properly. Stop being so indolent and start concentrating."

That was the last straw — the one that broke the camel's back. I screamed, "You're the indolent one — I've been doing all your work for you!"

He paused, and I actually thought I saw pain in his eyes. Softly he said, "It isn't proper, Dan, to yell at your teacher."

Too late I remembered that the purpose of his insults had always been to show me my own pride and resistance, and had taught me to persevere. But before I could apologize, Soc said, "Dan it's time we separated — at least for a time. You may come back once you have learned courtesy — and how to breathe properly. The one will help the other."

Sadly, I shuffled out, my head down, my world in darkness. Not until now had I realized how fond of him I had grown — and how grateful I felt. As I walked, I considered how patient he had been with my tantrums, complaints, and questions. I vowed never to yell at him in anger again.

Alone now, I tried harder than ever to correct my tense patterns of breathing, but it only seemed to get worse. If I breathed deeply, I'd forget to relax my shoulders; if I remembered to relax, I'd slouch over.

One week later, I went back to the station to see Soc and ask for his advice. I found him tinkering in the garage. He took one look at me and pointed to the door. Angry and hurt, I turned to limp off into the night. I heard his voice behind me. "After you learn how to breathe, do something about your sense of humor." His laughter taunted me halfway home.

When I reached the front steps of my apartment, I sat and gazed at the church across the street without really seeing anything in front of my eyes. I said to myself, "I'm going to quit this impossible training." But I didn't believe a word of it. I continued eating my salads, avoiding every temptation; I struggled doggedly with my breathing.

Nearly a month later, in midsummer, I remembered the café. I'd been so busy with studies and gymnastics by day and with Soc at night that I hadn't made time to visit Joseph. Now, I thought sadly, my nights were completely free. I walked to his café just at closing time. The place was empty; I found Joseph in the kitchen, carefully cleaning the fine porcelain dishes.

We were so different, Joseph and I. I was short, muscular, athletic, with short hair and a clean-shaven face; Joseph was tall, lean, even fragile looking, with a soft, curly blond beard. I moved and talked quickly; he did everything with slow-motion care. In spite of our differences, or maybe because of them, I was drawn to him.

We talked into the night as I helped him stack chairs and sweep the floors. Even as I talked, I concentrated as well as I could on my breathing, which made me drop a dish and trip over the carpet.

"Joseph," I asked, "did Socrates really make you go on 100-mile runs?"

He laughed. "No, Dan. My temperament isn't really suited for athletic feats. Didn't Soc tell you? I was his cook and personal attendant for years."

"Soc rarely speaks about his past. How could you have been his attendant for years? You couldn't be older than thirty-five."

Joseph beamed. "A bit older than that — I'm fifty-two."

"Are you serious?"

He nodded. There certainly was something to all those disciplines.

"But if you didn't do much physical conditioning, what was your training?"

"I was an angry, self-centered young man. And Soc kept asking me to do this, then that. I almost left many times, but I finally learned how to give, to help, to serve. He showed me the way to happiness and peace."

"What better place to learn how to serve," I said, "than at a service station."

Smiling, Joseph said, "He wasn't always a service station attendant, you know. His life has been extremely unusual and varied."

"Tell me about it!" I urged.

Joseph paused. "Socrates will tell you in his own way, his own time."

"I don't even know where he lives."

Scratching his head, Joseph said, "Come to think of it, I don't either."

Hiding my disappointment, I asked, "Did you call him Socrates, too? It seems an unlikely coincidence."

"No, but his new name, like his new student, has spirit." He smiled.

"You said he made rigorous demands on you."

"Yes, very rigorous. Nothing I did was good enough — and if he caught me moping or grumbling, he would send me off for weeks."

"I guess I'm an expert at both," I said. "He sent me away indefinitely."

"Why so?"

"He said I had to stay away until I could breathe properly — whatever that means."

"Ah, that," he said, putting down his broom. He came over to me and put one hand on my belly, one on my chest. "Now breathe," he said.

I started breathing slowly and deeply, the way Socrates had shown me. "No, don't try so hard." After a few minutes I started to feel funny in my belly and chest. They were warm inside, relaxed, and open. Suddenly I was crying like a baby, wildly happy and not knowing why. In that moment, I was breathing completely without effort; it felt like I was *being breathed*. It felt so pleasurable, I thought, Who needs to go to the movies to be entertained? I was so excited I could hardly contain myself! Then I felt the breathing start to tighten again.

"Joseph, I lost it!"

"Don't worry, Dan. You just need to relax into life a little more. Now that you know what natural breathing feels like, you'll *let* yourself breathe naturally, more and more, until it starts to feel normal. The breath is a bridge between mind and body, feeling and doing. Balanced, natural breathing brings you back to the present moment."

"Will that make me happy?"

"That will make you sane," he said.

"Joseph," I said, hugging him, "I don't know how you did what you did, but thank you — thank you so much."

He flashed that smile that made me feel warm all over and putting away his broom said, "Give my regards to...Socrates."

My breathing didn't improve right away. I still struggled. But one afternoon, on the way home from the weight room, I noticed that without my trying, my breathing was full and free — close to the way it felt at the café.

That night I burst into the office, ready to regale Socrates with my success and apologize for my behavior. He looked like he'd been expecting me. As I skidded to a halt in front of him, he said calmly, "OK, let's continue" — as if I'd just returned from the bathroom, rather than from six weeks of intensive training.

"Have you nothing else to say, Soc? No, 'Well done, lad,' no 'looking good'?"

"There's no praise and no blame on the path you've chosen. It's time you blew into your own sails."

I shook my head in exasperation, then smiled. At least I was back.

After that, when I wasn't cleaning toilets, I was learning new and more frustrating exercises, like meditating on internal sounds until I could hear several at once. One night, as I practiced that exercise, I found myself drawn into a state of profound peace unlike any I'd known before. For a period of time — I don't know how long — I felt as if I was out of my body. This marked the first time that my own efforts and energy resulted in a paranormal experience; I hadn't needed Soc's fingers pressing into my head, or hypnosis, or whatever he'd done.

Excited, I told him about it. Instead of congratulating me, he said, "Don't get distracted by your experiences. Experiences come and go; if you want experiences, go to the movies; it's easier than all these yogas — and you get popcorn. Meditate all day, if you like; hear sounds and see lights, or see sounds and hear lights. But don't get seduced by experience. Let it all go!"

Frustrated, I said, "I'm only 'experiencing,' as you call it, because you told me to!"

Socrates looked at me as if surprised. "Do I have to tell you everything?"

After a moment of exquisite anger, I found myself laughing. He laughed, too, pointing at me. "Dan, you just experienced an alchemical transformation — you just transmuted anger to laughter. This means your energy level is much higher than before. Barriers are breaking down. Maybe you're making a little progress after all." We were still chuckling when he handed me the mop.

The following night, for the first time, Socrates was completely silent about my behavior. I got the message: I was going to have to be responsible for watching myself from now on. That's when I realized the kindness in all of his criticisms. I almost missed them.

I wouldn't realize it until months later, but that evening, Socrates had stopped being my "parent" and became my friend.

I decided to pay Joseph a visit and tell him what had happened. As I walked down Shattuck a couple of fire engines wailed by me. I didn't think anything about it until I neared the café and saw the orange sky. I began to run.

The crowd was already dispersing when I arrived. Joseph had just arrived himself and was standing in front of his charred and gutted café. I heard his cry of anguish and saw him drop slowly to his knees and cry. By the time I reached him, his face was serene.

The fire chief came over to him and told him that the fire had probably started at the dry cleaners next door. "Thank you," Joseph said.

"Joseph, I'm so sorry."

"Yes, me too," he replied with a smile.

"But a few moments ago you were so upset."

He smiled. "Yes, I was." I remembered Soc's words, "Let feelings flow, then let them go." Until now, this had seemed like a nice concept, but here, before the blackened, waterlogged remains of his beautiful café, this gentle warrior had demonstrated how to make peace with emotions.

"It was such a beautiful place, Joseph," I sighed, shaking my head.

"Yes," he said wistfully, "wasn't it?"

For some reason, his calm now bothered me. "Aren't you upset at all?"

He looked at me dispassionately, then said, "I have a story you might enjoy, Dan. Want to hear it?"

"Well — OK."

In a small fishing village in Japan, there lived a young, unmarried woman who gave birth to a child. Her parents felt disgraced and demanded to know the identity of the father. Afraid, she refused to tell them. The fisherman she loved had told her, secretly, that he was going off to seek his fortune and would return to marry her. Her parents persisted. In desperation, she named Hakuin, a monk who lived in the hills, as the father.

Outraged, the parents took the infant girl up to his door, pounded until he opened it, and handed him the baby, saying, "This child is yours; you must care for it!"

"Is that so?" Hakuin said, taking the child in his arms, waving good-bye to the parents.

A year passed and the real father returned to marry the woman. At once they went to Hakuin to beg for the return of the child. "We must have our daughter," they said.

"Is that so?" said Hakuin, handing the child to them.

Joseph smiled and waited for my response.

"An interesting story, Joseph, but I don't understand why you're telling it to me now. I mean, your café just burned down!"

"Is that so?" he said. Then we laughed as I shook my head in resignation.

"Joseph, you're as crazy as Socrates."

"Why, thank you, Dan — and you're upset enough for both of us. Don't worry about me, though; I've been ready for a change. I'll probably move south soon — or north. It makes no difference."

"Well, don't go without saying good-bye."

"Good-bye, then," he said, giving me one of his bear hugs. "I'll be leaving tomorrow."

"Are you going to say good-bye to Socrates?"

He laughed, replying, "Socrates and I rarely say hello or good-bye. You'll understand later." With that, we parted.

About 3:00 A.M. Friday morning I passed the clock at Shattuck and Center on my way to the gas station. I was more aware than ever of how much I still had to learn. I stepped into the office already talking a mile a minute. "Socrates, Joseph's café burned down. He's going away."

"Strange," he said, "cafés usually burn *up*." He was making jokes. "Anyone hurt?" he asked, without apparent concern.

"Not that I know of. Did you hear me, aren't you even a little upset?"

"Was Joseph upset?"

"Well…yes and no."

"Well, there you are." And that topic was simply closed.

Then, to my amazement, Socrates took out a pack of cigarettes and lit one. "Speaking of smoke," he said, "did I ever mention to you that there's no such thing as a bad habit?"

I couldn't believe my eyes or my ears. This isn't happening, I told myself.

"No, you didn't, and I've gone to great lengths on your recommendation to change my bad habits."

"That was to develop your will, you see, and to give your instincts a refresher course. You see, any unconscious, compulsive ritual is a problem. But specific activities — smoking, drinking, taking drugs, eating sweets, or asking silly questions — are both bad and good; every action has its price, and its pleasures. Recognizing both sides, you become realistic and responsible for your actions. And only then can you make the warrior's free and conscious choice — to do or not to do.

"There is a saying: 'When you sit, sit; when you stand, stand; whatever you do, don't wobble.' Once you make your choice, do it with all your spirit. Don't be like the preacher who thought about praying while making love to his wife, and thought about making love to his wife while praying."

I laughed at this image, while Socrates blew perfect smoke rings.

"It's better to make a mistake with the full force of your

being than to timidly avoid mistakes with a trembling spirit. Responsibility means recognizing both pleasure and price, action and consequence, then making a choice."

"It sounds so 'either-or.' What about moderation?"

"Moderation?" He leaped up on the desk, like an evangelist. "Moderation? It's mediocrity, fear, and confusion in disguise. It's the devil's dilemma. It's neither doing nor not doing. It's the wobbling compromise that makes no one happy. Moderation is for the bland, the apologetic, for the fence-sitters of the world afraid to take a stand. It's for those afraid to laugh or cry, for those afraid to live or die. *Moderation*" — he took a deep breath, getting ready for his final condemnation — "is *lukewarm tea,* the devil's own brew!"

"But you've told me the value of balance, the middle way, the golden mean."

Socrates scratched his head. "Well, you have a good point there. Maybe it's time to trust your own inner knower, the counsel of your own heart."

Laughing, I said, "Your sermons come in like a lion and go out like a lamb, Soc. You'll have to keep practicing."

He shrugged his shoulders, climbing down from the desk. "They always told me that in the seminary." I didn't know whether he was kidding or not.

"Anyway," I said, "I still think smoking is disgusting."

"Haven't I got the message across to you *yet?* Smoking is not disgusting; only the *habit* is. I may enjoy a cigarette, then not smoke again for six months. And when I do smoke, I don't pretend that my lungs won't pay a price; I follow appropriate action afterward to help counterbalance the negative effects."

"I just never expected a warrior like you would ever smoke."

He blew smoke rings at me. "I don't live according to anyone's expectations, Dan — not even my own. Nor do all warriors act exactly as I do. But we must all follow the House Rules, you see.

"So whether or not my behavior meets your new standards, it should be clear to you that I have no compulsions or habits. My actions are conscious, spontaneous, intentional, and complete."

Socrates put out his cigarette, smiling at me. "You've become too stuffy, with all your pride and superior discipline. It's time we did a little celebrating."

Then Socrates pulled out a bottle of gin from his desk. I just sat in disbelief, shaking my head. He mixed me a drink with gin and soda pop.

"Soda pop?" I asked.

"Only have fruit juice here. And don't call me 'Pop,'" he said, reminding me of the words he'd spoken to me so long before. Now here he was, offering me a gin-and-ginger ale, drinking his straight.

"So," he said, tossing down the gin, "time to party, no holds barred."

"I like your enthusiasm, Soc, but I have a hard workout tomorrow."

"Get your coat, sonny, and follow me." I did.

The only thing I remember clearly that Saturday night in San Francisco is that we started early and never stopped. The evening was a blur of lights, tinkling glasses, and laughter.

I do remember Sunday morning. It was about five o'clock. My head was throbbing. We were walking down Mission, crossing Fourth Street. I could barely see the street signs through the thick early morning fog that had rolled in. Suddenly, Soc stopped and stared into the fog. I stumbled into him, giggled, then woke up quickly; something was wrong. A large dark shape emerged from the mist. My half-forgotten dream flashed into my mind but vanished as I saw another shape, then a third: three men. Two of them — tall, lean, tense — blocked our way. The third approached us and drew a stiletto from his worn leather jacket. I felt my pulse pounding through my temples.

"Give me your money," he commanded.

Not thinking clearly, I stepped toward him, reaching for my wallet, and stumbled forward.

He was startled and rushed toward me, slashing with his knife. Socrates, moving faster than I'd ever seen before, caught the man's wrist, whirled around, and threw him into the street, just as another thug lunged for me. He never touched me;

Socrates had kicked his legs out from under him with a lightning sweep. Before the third attacker could even move, Soc was upon him, taking him down with a wristlock and a sweeping motion of his arm. He sat down on the man and said, "Don't you think you ought to consider nonviolence?"

One of the men started to get up when Socrates let out a powerful shout and the man fell backward. By then the leader had picked himself out of the street, found his knife, and was limping furiously toward Socrates. Socrates stood up, lifted the man he'd been sitting on, and threw him toward the knifeman, yelling, "Catch!" They tumbled to the concrete; then, in a wild rage, all three came screaming at us in a last desperate assault.

The next few minutes were blurred. I remember being pushed by Socrates and falling. Then it was quiet, except for a moan. Socrates stood still, then shook his arms loose and took a deep breath. He threw the knives into the sewer. Then he turned to me. "You OK?"

"Except for my head."

"You get hit?"

"Only by alcohol. What happened?"

He turned to the three men stretched out on the pavement, knelt, and felt their pulses. Turning them over, almost tenderly, he gave gentle prodding motions, checking them for injuries. Only then did I realize he was doing his best to heal them! "Call an ambulance," he said, turning to me. I ran to a nearby phone booth and called. Then we left and walked quickly to the bus station. I looked at Socrates. There were faint tears in his eyes, and for the first time since I'd known him, he looked pale and very tired.

We spoke little on the bus ride home. That was fine with me; talking hurt too much. When the bus stopped at University and Shattuck, Socrates got off and said, "You're invited to my office next Wednesday, for a few drinks... " Smiling at my pained expression, he continued, " ...of herb tea."

I got off the bus a block from home. My head was ready to explode. I felt like we'd lost the fight, and they were still beating on my head. I tried to keep my eyes closed as much as possible, walking the last block to the apartment house. So this is what it feels like to be a vampire, I thought. Sunlight *can* kill.

Our celebration had taught me two things: first, that I had needed to loosen up and let go; second, that heavy drinking, at least for me, wasn't worth the price. Besides, the pleasure was insignificant compared to what I was beginning to enjoy.

Monday's gymnastics workout was a struggle; still, there was a chance that I might somehow get ready in time. My leg was healing better than I'd had any right to expect; I had been taken under the wings of an extraordinary man.

Walking home, I was so overwhelmed with gratitude that I knelt outside my apartment and touched the earth. Taking a handful of dirt in my hand, I gazed up through emerald leaves shimmering in the breeze. For a few precious seconds, I seemed to slowly melt into the earth. Then, for the first time since I was a young boy, I felt a life-giving Presence without a name.

Then my analytical mind piped in: Wow! A spontaneous mystical experience. The spell was broken. I returned to my earthly predicament — an ordinary man, standing under an elm, holding dirt in his hand. In a relaxed daze, I entered my apartment, read for a while, and fell asleep.

Tuesday was a day of quiet — the quiet before the storm.

Wednesday morning I plunged into the mainstream of classes. My feelings of serenity, which I thought were permanent, soon gave way to subtle anxieties and old urges. After all my disciplined training, I was profoundly disappointed. Then something new happened — a powerful intuitive message came to me: Old urges continue to arise, but urges do not matter; only actions do. A warrior is as a warrior does.

At first, I thought my mind was playing tricks on me. But it wasn't a thought or a voice; it was a *feeling-certainty,* a *knowing.* It was as if Socrates was inside me, a warrior within. This feeling was to remain with me.

That evening, I went to the station to tell Socrates about my mind's recent hyperactivity, and about the Feeling. I found him replacing a generator in a battered Mercury. He looked up, greeted me, and said casually, "I heard that Joseph died this morning."

I fell back against a station wagon behind me, shocked by the news of Joseph's death — and by Soc's callousness. Finally, I was able to speak. "How did he die?"

"Very well, I imagine. He had leukemia, you see. A rare form. Had been ill for a number of years; he hung in there for a long time. A fine warrior, that one." He spoke with affection, but without apparent sorrow.

"Socrates, aren't you upset, just a little?"

He laid the wrench down. "That reminds me of a story I heard a long time ago, about a mother who was overcome with grief by the death of her young son.

"'I can't bear the pain and sorrow,' she told her sister.

"'My sister, did you mourn your son before he was born?'

"'No, of course not,' the despondent woman replied.

"'Well then, you need not mourn for him now. He has only returned to the same place, his original home, before he was ever born.'"

"Is that story a comfort to you, Socrates?"

"Well, I think it's a good story. Perhaps in time you'll appreciate it," he replied brightly.

"I thought I knew you well, Socrates, but I never knew you could be so heartless."

"No cause for worry, Dan — death is perfectly safe."

"But he's gone!"

Soc laughed softly. "Maybe he's gone, maybe not. Maybe he was never here!" His laughter rang through the garage.

I suddenly realized why I was so troubled. "Would you feel the same way if I had died?"

"Of course!" He laughed. "Dan, there are things you don't yet understand. For now, just think of death as a transformation — a bit more radical than puberty, but nothing to get particularly upset about. It's just one of the body's changes. When it happens, it happens. The warrior neither seeks death nor flees from it."

His face grew more somber before he spoke again. "Death is not sad; the sad thing is that most people don't really live at all." That's when his eyes filled with tears. We sat, two friends in silence, before I headed home.

I had just turned down a side street, when the Feeling came again: Tragedy is very different for the warrior and for the fool. Socrates simply didn't consider Joseph's death a tragedy. I wasn't to realize why that was so until months later, deep within a mountain cave.

I couldn't shake the belief that Socrates and I were supposed to be miserable when death struck. Confused and unsettled, I reached home and finally fell asleep.

In the morning, I understood: Socrates had simply not met my expectations. I saw the futility of trying to live up to anyone else's expectations, including my own. I would, as a peaceful warrior, choose when, where, and how I would behave. With that commitment, I began to live the life of a warrior.

That night, I walked into the station office and said to Socrates, "I'm ready. Nothing will stop me."

His fierce stare undid all my months of training. I quivered. He whispered, yet his voice seemed piercing. "You sound like a fool. No one knows his readiness until the time comes. You don't have much time left! Each day that passes is one day closer to your death. We are not playing games here, do you understand that?"

The wind began to howl outside. Without warning, I felt his fingers grasp my temples.

I was crouched in the brush. Ten feet away, facing my hiding place, was a swordsman, over seven feet tall. His massive, muscular body reeked of sulfur. His head, even his forehead, was covered by ugly, matted hair; his eyebrows were huge slashes on a hateful, twisted face.

He stared malevolently at a young swordsman who faced him. Five identical images of the giant materialized and encircled the young swordsman. All six of them laughed at once — a groaning, growling laugh, deep in their bellies. I felt sick.

The young warrior jerked his head right and left, swinging his sword frantically, whirling, dodging, and cutting through the air. He didn't have a chance.

With a roar, all the images leaped toward him. Behind him, the giant's sword cut downward, hacking off his arm. He screamed in pain as the blood spurted, and slashed blindly through the air in a last frenzied effort. The huge sword sliced again, and the young swordsman's head fell from his shoulders and rolled to the earth, a shocked expression on its face.

"Ohhh," I groaned involuntarily, nausea washing over me. The stink of sulfur overwhelmed me. A painful grip on my arm tore me from the bushes and flung me to the ground. When I opened my eyes, the dead eyes of the young swordsman's severed head, inches away from my face, silently warned me of my own impending doom. Then I heard the guttural voice of the giant.

"Say farewell to life, young fool!" the magician growled. His taunt enraged me. I dove for the young warrior's sword and rolled to my feet, facing him. With a scream he attacked.

I parried, but the force of his blow knocked me off my feet. Then, suddenly, there were six of him. I tried to keep my eye on the original as I leaped to my feet, but was no longer sure.

They began a chant, deep in their bellies; it became a low-pitched, horrible death rattle as they crept slowly toward me.

Then the Feeling came to me and I knew what I had to do. *The giant represents the* source *of all your woes; he is your* mind. *He is the demon you must cut through. Don't be deluded like the fallen warrior: keep your focus!* Absurdly I thought, One hell of a time for a lesson. Then I was back to my immediate predicament.

Feeling an icy calm, I lay down on my back and closed my eyes, as if surrendering to my fate, the sword in my hands, its blade across my chest and cheek. The illusions could fool my eyes but not my ears. Only the real swordsman would make a sound as he walked. I heard him behind me. He had only two choices — to walk away, or to kill. He chose to kill. I listened intently. Just as I sensed his sword about to cut downward, I drove my blade upward with all my might and felt it pierce, tearing upward through cloth, flesh, muscle. A terrible scream, and I heard the thud of his body. Face down, impaled on my sword, was the demon.

"You almost didn't come back that time," said Socrates, his brow knitted.

I ran to the bathroom, where I was thoroughly sick. When I came out, Soc had made some chamomile tea with licorice, "for the nerves and the stomach."

I started to tell Socrates about the journey. "I was hiding in the bush behind you, watching the whole thing," he interrupted. "I nearly sneezed once; sure glad I didn't. I certainly wasn't anxious to tangle with that character. For a moment, I thought I was going to have to step in, but you handled yourself pretty well, Dan."

"Well, thanks, Soc."

"But you seemed to have missed the point that nearly cost you your life."

Now it was my turn to interrupt him. "The main point I was concerned with was at the end of that giant's blade. Anyway, I didn't miss it."

"Is that so?"

"Soc, I've been battling illusions my whole life, preoccupied with every petty personal problem. I've dedicated my life to self-improvement without grasping the one problem that sent me seeking in the first place. While trying to make everything in the world work out for me, I kept getting sucked back into my own mind, always preoccupied with me, me, me. That giant was me — the ego, the little self — who I've always believed myself to be. And I cut through it!"

"No doubt about that," he said.

"What would have happened if the giant had won; what then?"

"Don't talk of such things," he said darkly.

"I have to know. Would I have really died?"

"Possibly," he said. "At the very least, you would have gone mad."

Just then the teakettle began to shriek.

CHAPTER FIVE

THE MOUNTAIN PATH

Socrates poured steaming hot tea into our twin mugs and spoke the first encouraging words I'd heard in many months. "Your survival in the duel means that you're ready for the next step toward the One Goal."

"What's that?"

"When you discover that, you'll already be there. In the meantime, your training can now move to a different arena."

A change. A sign of progress! I was getting excited. Finally we're going to get moving again, I thought. "Socrates," I asked, "what new arena?"

"For one thing you're going to have to find the answers from within. Beginning now — go out back, behind the station, behind the trash bin. There, in the corner of the lot, against the wall, you'll find a large flat stone. Sit on that stone until you have something of value to tell me."

I paused. "That's it?"

"That's it. Sit and wait until you have an insight worth sharing."

I went outside, found the rock, and sat in the darkness. First, random thoughts drifted through my mind. I thought of all the important concepts I'd learned in my years at school. An hour went by, then two, then three. The sun would rise in another few hours, and I was getting cold. I began to slow my breathing and to vividly imagine my belly as warm. Before long, I felt comfortable again.

Dawn came. The only thing that I could think of to tell him was a realization I'd had during a psychology lecture. I stood up on stiff, sore legs and hobbled into the office. Socrates, looking relaxed and comfortable at his desk, said, "Ah, so soon? Well, what is it?"

I was almost embarrassed to say it but hoped he'd be satisfied. "OK, Soc. Beneath all our apparent differences we share the same human needs and fears; we're all on the same path together, guiding one another. And this understanding brings compassion."

"Not bad. Back to the rock."

"But it's morning — you're leaving."

"That's no problem." He grinned. "I'm sure you'll have thought of something by tonight."

"Tonight? But I..." He pointed out the door.

Sitting on the rock, my whole body aching, I reflected on my childhood and searched my past, reaching for insights. Nothing came. Then I tried to compress all that had transpired in the months with Socrates into a witty aphorism.

I thought of the classes I was missing and the excuse I'd have to give the coach. What would I say? That I'd been sitting on a rock in a gas station? That would sound crazy enough to make him laugh.

The sun crept with agonizing slowness across the sky. I sat hungry, irritated, and depressed, as darkness fell. I had nothing for Socrates. Then, just as he was due back, it came to me. He wanted something deeper, more cosmic. I concentrated harder. I saw Socrates enter the office, waving to me. I redoubled my efforts. Then, about midnight, I had it. I couldn't even walk, so I stretched for a few minutes before shuffling into the office.

"All right, Socrates. I've got it. So far I've seen beneath people's social masks to their common fears and troubled minds, but that has only made me cynical, because I haven't yet looked still deeper to find the light within them." I figured this was a revelation of major proportions.

"Excellent," he announced. Just as I started to settle onto

the sofa with a sigh, he added, "But not quite what I had in mind. Can't you bring me something more moving?" I roared with frustration and stomped out to my philosopher's stone.

"Something more moving," he had said. Was that a hint? I naturally thought back to my recent workouts in the gymnastics room where my teammates now clucked about me like mother hens, worried that I might reinjure myself. Recently I was doing giant swings around the high bar, missed a pirouette change, and had to jump off from the top of the bar. I knew I was going to land on my feet pretty hard, but before I even hit the ground, Sid and Herb caught me in midair and set me down gently. "Be careful, Dan!" Sid scolded. "You want to snap your leg again?"

But none of that seemed relevant to my present quandary. So I let my awareness relax, hoping that maybe the Feeling would advise me. Nothing came. I was so stiff and sore I couldn't concentrate anymore. So I stood up slowly and began to practice a few flowing movements of T'ai Chi, the Chinese form of slow-motion exercise that Soc had shown me. As I bent my knees and gracefully rocked back and forth, my arms floating in the air, I let my breath flow with the shifting of my weight. My mind emptied, then filled with a scene:

A few days before, I had jogged slowly and carefully to Provo Square, in the middle of Berkeley, across from City Hall and directly adjacent to Berkeley High School. To help relax, I began swaying back and forth in the movements of T'ai Chi. I concentrated on softness and balance, feeling like seaweed floating in the ocean.

I noticed a few boys and girls from the high school stop to watch me, before I returned my attention to the body, letting my awareness flow with the movements. When I finished the routine, I picked up my sweatpants and started to slip them back on over my running shorts. Just then my attention was captured by two pretty teenagers who were watching me and giggling. I guess those girls are impressed, I thought, as I put both legs into one pant leg, lost my balance, tipped over, and sprawled on the grass.

A few other students joined the girls in their laughter. I felt embarrassed for a moment, but then lay back and laughed with them.

I wondered, still standing on the rock, why that incident came to me. Then it hit me; I walked into the office, stood before Soc's desk, and announced, *"There are no ordinary moments!"*

Soc smiled. "Welcome back." I collapsed on the couch and he made tea.

After that, I treated every moment in the gym — on the ground as well as in the air — as special, worthy of my full attention. But as Socrates had explained to me more than once, the ability to extend razor-sharp attention to every moment in my daily life would require much more practice.

The next day, in the early afternoon before workout, I took advantage of the blue sky and warm sunshine to sit in the redwood grove and meditate. I hadn't been sitting for more than ten minutes when someone grabbed me and started shaking me back and forth. I rolled away, panting, and stood in a crouch. Then I saw my assailant. "Socrates, you have absolutely no manners!"

"Wake up!" he said. "No more sleeping on the job. There's work to be done."

"I'm off duty now," I teased. "Lunch hour — see the next clerk."

"Time to get moving, Sitting Bull. Go get your running shoes and meet me back here in twenty minutes."

I went home and put on my worn old sneakers, and hurried back to the redwood grove. Socrates was nowhere in sight. Then I saw her.

"Joy!" She was barefoot and wearing blue running shorts and a T-shirt tied at the waist. I ran up to her and hugged her. I laughed, I tried to push her, to wrestle her to the ground, but she was no pushover. I wanted to talk, to tell her my feelings, my plans. She just held her fingers to my lips and said, "Time to talk later, Danny. For now, just follow me."

She began a combination of T'ai Chi movements, calisthenics, and coordination exercises for the mind and the body. In a few minutes, I felt light, loose, and energized.

Without warning, Joy said, "On your mark, get set, go!" She took off, running up through campus. I followed, straining to keep up as we headed toward the hills of Strawberry Canyon. Huffing and puffing, not yet in running shape, I began to trail far behind. I pushed harder, my lungs burning. Up ahead, Joy had stopped at the top of the rise overlooking the football stadium. I could hardly breathe by the time I reached her.

"What took you so long, sweetheart?" she said, hands on her hips. Then she bounced off again, up the canyon, heading for the base of the fire trails, narrow dirt roads that wound up through the hills. Doggedly I pursued her, hurting as I hadn't hurt in a long time but determined to run her down.

As we neared the trails, she slowed down and began running at a humane pace. Then, to my dismay, she reached the base of the lower trails and instead of turning around, led me up another grade, far into the hills.

I offered up a silent prayer of thanks as she turned around at the end of the lower trails, instead of heading up the steep, quarter-mile connector that joined the lower and upper trails. As we ran more easily back down a long grade, Joy began to talk. "Danny, Socrates asked me to introduce you to your new phase of training. Meditation is a useful practice, but eventually you have to open your eyes and look around. The warrior's life is a moving experience."

I had been listening thoughtfully, staring at the ground. I answered, "Yes, I understand that, Joy. That's why I train in gymnas..." I looked up just in time to see her lovely figure disappear in the distance.

Later that afternoon, I walked into the gym, lay on the mat, and stretched and stretched until the coach came over and asked, "Are you going to lie around all day, or would you like to try one of the other nice activities we have for you — we call them 'gymnastics' events."

I tried some simple tumbling moves for the first time, testing my leg. Running was one thing; tumbling was another.

And it hurt. Advanced moves could exert as much as sixteen hundred pounds of force as the legs drove into the ground, thrusting the body skyward. I also began to test my trampoline legs for the first time in a year. Bouncing rhythmically into the air, I somersaulted again and again. Pat and Dennis, my two trampoline mates, yelled, "Millman, will you take it easy? You know your leg isn't healed yet!" I wondered what they'd say if they knew I had just run for miles in the hills.

Walking to the station that night, I was so tired I could hardly keep my eyes open. I stepped out of the cool October air into the office, ready for some soothing tea and relaxing talk. I should have known better.

"Come over here and face me. Stand like this." Socrates bent his knees, thrust his hips forward, and pulled his shoulders back. Then he put his hands out in front of him as if holding an invisible beach ball. "Hold this position without moving. Breathe slowly, and listen up. You move well, Dan, compared to most people, but your muscles hold too much tension. Tense muscles require more energy to move. So you have to learn how to release stored tension."

My legs were starting to shake with pain and fatigue. "This hurts!"

"It only hurts because your muscles are like rocks."

"All right, you've made your point! How long do I have to stay this way?"

Socrates only smiled and left the office abruptly, leaving me standing bent-legged, sweating and shaking. He came back with a grizzled tomcat who had obviously seen some action on the front lines.

"You need to develop muscles like Oscar so that you can move like *us*," he said, scratching the purring feline behind the ears.

My forehead beaded with perspiration; intense pain gripped my shoulders and legs. Finally, Socrates said, "At ease." I straightened, wiping my forehead and shaking my arms. "Come over here and introduce yourself to Oscar." The cat purred with delight as Soc scratched him behind the ears. "We're both going to serve as your coaches, aren't we, boy?"

Oscar meowed loudly. I patted him. "Now squeeze his leg muscles, slowly, to the bone."

"I might hurt him."

"Squeeze!"

I pressed deeper and deeper into the cat's muscle until I felt the bone. The cat watched me with curiosity and kept purring.

"Now squeeze my calf muscle," Soc said.

"Oh, I couldn't, Soc. We don't know each other well enough."

"Do it, Dumbo." I squeezed and was surprised to feel that his muscles felt just like the cat's, yielding like firm jelly.

"Your turn," he said, reaching down and squeezing my calf muscle.

"Ow!" I yelped. "I'd always thought hard muscles were normal," I said, rubbing my calves.

"They are normal, Dan, but you must go far beyond normal, beyond the usual, common, or reasonable, to reach the realm of the warrior. You've always tried to become superior in an ordinary realm. Now you're going to become ordinary in a superior realm."

Socrates let Oscar go out the door. He then began my introduction to the subtle elements of physical training. "By now you can appreciate how the mind imposes tension on the body. Worries, anxieties, and other mental debris are stored as chronic tension. Now it's time for you to release these tensions and free your body from the past."

Socrates spread a white sheet on the carpet and told me to strip down to my shorts. He did the same. "What are you going to do if a customer comes?" He pointed to his overalls hanging by the door.

"Now, do exactly as I do." He began by rubbing a sweet-scented oil over his left foot. I copied every step as he squeezed, pressed, and dug very deeply into the bottom, top, sides, and between the toes, stretching, pressing, and pulling. "Massage the bones, not just the flesh and muscle — *deeper*," he said. Half an hour later, we were through with the left foot. We repeated the process with the right foot. This went on for hours, covering every part of the body. I learned things about my muscles, ligaments, and tendons I'd never known before. I could feel where they were attached; I could feel the shape of the bones. It was amazing that I, an athlete, was so unfamiliar with the inside of my body.

Socrates had quickly slipped into his overalls a few times when the bell clanged, but otherwise, we were undisturbed. When I donned my clothes at dawn, I felt as if I had a new body. Returning from a customer, Soc said, "You've cleaned many old fears from your body. Take the time to repeat this process once a week for the next month. Pay attention to the site of your injury."

More homework, I thought. The sky grew light. I yawned. Time to go home. As I was walking out the door, Socrates told me to be at the base of the fire trails at 1 P.M. sharp.

I arrived early at the trails. I stretched and warmed up lazily; my body felt loose and light after the "bone massage," but with only a few hours' sleep I was still tired. A light drizzle had begun; all in all, I didn't feel like running anywhere, with anyone today. Then I heard a rustling in the bushes nearby. I stood quietly and watched, expecting to see a deer emerge from the thicket. Out of the foliagé stepped Joy, again barefoot, looking like an elf princess, wearing dark green shorts and a lime T-shirt emblazoned with the words "Happiness is a full tank." A gift from Socrates, no doubt.

"Hey, Joy, good to see you. Let's sit down and talk; there's so much I want to tell you." She smiled and sped away.

As I pursued her up around the first curve, almost slipping on the wet clay earth, I felt a weakness in my legs after yesterday's exercise. I was soon winded, grateful that she kept her pace slower than yesterday's.

We approached the end of the lower trail. My breathing was labored and my leg throbbed. Then she said, "Upsy daisy," and started up the connector. My mind rebelled. My weary muscles resisted. Then I looked up at Joy, bounding lightly up the hill as if it were level.

With a yell, I started up the connector. Like a drunken gorilla, I ran hunched over, grunting, panting, blindly clambering up, two steps forward, sliding one step back.

At the top, the trail leveled off. Joy stood there, smelling the wet pine needles, looking as peaceful and content as Bambi. My lungs begged for more air. "I have an idea," I panted. "Let's walk the rest of the way — no, let's crawl — it gives us more time to talk. How does that sound, pretty good?"

"Let's go," she said merrily.

My chagrin turned to anger. I'd run her to the ends of the earth! I stepped into a puddle, slipped through the mud, and ran into a small tree branch, nearly knocking myself over the side of the hill. "Goddamn-it-shit-son-of-a-bitch!" My words emerged a hoarse whisper. I had no energy left to talk.

I struggled over a small hill that seemed like the Colorado Rockies and saw Joy squatting, playing with some wild rabbits as they hopped across the trail. When I stumbled up to her, the rabbits leaped into the bushes. Joy looked up at me, smiling, and said, "Oh, there you are." By some heroic effort, I leaned forward and managed to accelerate past her, but she just shot ahead and disappeared again.

We had climbed eleven hundred feet. I was now high above the bay and could see the university below me. I was, however, in no condition or state of mind to appreciate the view. I felt very close to passing out. I had a vision of me buried on the hill, under the wet earth, with a marker: "Here lies Dan. Nice guy, good try."

The rain had increased, but I ran on as if in a trance, leaning forward, stumbling, pulling one leg forward after the other. My shoes felt like iron boots. Then I rounded a corner and saw a final grade that looked nearly vertical. Again my mind refused; my body stopped, but up there, at the top of the hill, stood Joy, with her hands on her hips as if challenging me. Somehow I managed to tip forward and start my legs moving again. I plodded, I pushed, I strained and groaned up the last endless steps until I ran right into her.

"Whoa, boy, whoa," she laughed. "You're finished, all done."

Between gasps, as I leaned against her, I wheezed, "You... can...say...that...again."

We walked back down the hill, giving me welcome time to

recover and talk. "Joy, it seems like pushing this hard this fast isn't natural. I wasn't really prepared to run this far; I don't think it's very good for the body."

"Probably not," she said. "But this wasn't a test of your body; it was a test of your spirit — a test to see if you could push on — not just with the hill, but with your training. If you had stopped, it would have been the end. But you passed, Danny, you passed with flying colors."

The wind began to blow, and the rain poured down, drenching us. Then Joy stopped, took my head in her hands, and kissed me. Water dripped from our sopping hair and ran down our cheeks. I reached around her waist and was drawn into her shining eyes, and we kissed again.

I was filled with a new energy. I laughed at the way we both looked, like sponges that needed to be wrung out, and said, "I'll race you to the bottom!" I took off and got a good head start. "What the hell," I figured. "I can *slide* down these damn trails!" She won, of course.

Later that afternoon, dry and warm, I stretched lazily in the gym with Sid, Gary, Scott, and Herb. The warmth of the gym was a pleasurable shelter from the pounding rain outside. Despite my grueling run, I still had energy to spare.

But by the time I stepped into the office that evening and took off my shoes, my reserves had evaporated. I wanted to flop my aching body down on the couch and take a nap for ten or twelve hours. Resisting the urge, I sat as gracefully as I could manage and faced Socrates.

I was amused to see that he'd rearranged the decor. Pictures of golfers, skiers, tennis players, and gymnasts were up on the wall; on his desk sat a baseball mitt and a football. Socrates even wore a sweatshirt that said, "Ohio State Coaching Staff." It seemed that we'd entered the sports phase of my training.

While Soc made us some of his special wake-up tea he called "Thundering Tarnation," I told him about my gymnastics progress. He listened attentively, then said, "There is more to gymnastics and other sports than most people appreciate."

"What do you mean?"

He reached into his desk and took out three lethal-looking

daggers. "Uh, never mind, Soc," I said, "I don't really need an explanation."

"Stand up," he ordered. When I did, he casually threw a knife, underhand, straight toward my chest.

I leaped aside, falling onto the couch as the knife dropped soundlessly to the carpet. I lay there, shocked, my heart beating overtime.

"Good," he said. "You overreacted a bit, but good. Now stand up and catch the next one."

Just then, the kettle started whistling. "Oh, well," I said, rubbing my sweaty palms together, "time for tea."

"It will keep," he said. "Watch me closely." Soc tossed a glittering blade straight into the air. I watched it spin and drop. As it fell, he matched the speed of the blade with the downward motion of his hand and grasped the handle between his thumb and fingers, like a pincer, gripping firmly.

"Now you try. Notice how I caught it so that even if I happened to grab the blade, it wouldn't slice me." He tossed another knife toward me. More relaxed, I stepped out of the way and made only a feeble attempt at catching it.

"If you drop the next one, I'm going to start throwing overhand," he warned.

This time my eyes were glued to the handle; as it came near, I reached out. "Hey, I did it!"

"Aren't sports fun?" he said. We became totally immersed in throwing and catching. Then finally we sat down for tea.

"Now let me tell you about *satori,* a Zen concept. Satori occurs when attention rests in the present moment, when the body is alert, sensitive, relaxed, and the emotions are open and free. Satori is what you experienced when the knife was flying toward you. Satori is the warrior's state of being."

"You know, Soc, I've had that feeling many times, especially during competitions. Often I'm concentrating so hard, I don't even hear the applause."

"Yes, that is the experience of satori. Sports, dance, or music, and any other challenging activity can serve as a gateway to satori. You imagine that you love gymnastics, but it's merely the wrapping for the gift of satori. Your gymnastics requires full attention on your actions. Gymnastics draws you into the moment of truth; your life is on the line. As with a dueling samurai, it's satori or death."

"Like in the middle of a double somersault."

"Yes. And this is why gymnastics is one of the warrior's arts, a way to focus the mind and free the emotions as you train the body. But most athletes fail to expand this clarity into daily life. This is your task. And when satori becomes your everyday reality, we will be equals. Satori is your key to the gate."

I sighed. "It seems like such a distant possibility, Socrates."

"When you ran up the hill after Joy, you didn't just gaze wistfully at the top of the mountain, you looked directly in front of you and took one step at a time. That's how it works."

"The House Rules, right?"

Socrates nodded, smiling. "And now you'd better get some sleep. Special session tomorrow morning at 7:00. Berkeley High School track."

When my alarm rang at 6:15, I dragged myself out of bed, submerged my head in cold water, did some deep breathing exercises, then screamed into my pillow to wake up.

I was alert by the time I hit the streets. I jogged slowly, crossing Shattuck, and cut down Allston Way past the Berkeley YMCA, the post office, then across Milvia, onto the high school grounds, where Soc was waiting.

His special program started with a half hour in that unbearable crouching position he'd shown me in the gas station. Then he showed me some basic principles of the martial arts. "The true martial arts teach nonresistance — the way of the trees bending in the wind. This attitude is far more important than physical technique."

Using the principles of aikido, Socrates was able to throw me without any apparent effort, no matter how I tried to push him, grab him, punch him, or even tackle him. "Never struggle with anyone or anything. When you're pushed, pull; when you're pulled, push. Find the natural course and bend with it. Join with nature's power." His actions proved his words.

Soon it was time to go. "See you tomorrow, same time, same place. Stay home tonight and practice your exercises.

146

Remember to breathe so slowly that you wouldn't disturb a feather in front of your nose." He glided off as if on roller skates, and I ran toward my apartment, so relaxed that I felt like the wind was blowing me home.

In the gym I did my best to apply what I'd learned, "letting movements happen" instead of trying to do them. My giant swings on the high bar seemed to go around by themselves; I swung, hopped, and somersaulted to handstand after handstand on the parallel bars; my circles, scissors, and pommel work on the horse felt as if I were supported by strings from the ceiling, weightless. And, finally, my legs were regaining their spring.

Soc and I met just after sunrise every morning. I would stride along, and he would run leaping like a gazelle. Each day I grew more relaxed and my reflexes became lightning quick.

One day, when we were in the middle of our warm-up run, he suddenly stopped, looking paler than I'd ever seen him before.

"I'd better sit down," he said.

"Socrates, are you OK?"

"Just keep running, Dan. I'll sit quietly." I did as he asked, but kept my eyes on him, sitting with eyes closed looking proud and straight, but older somehow.

As we'd agreed weeks before, I no longer came to see Socrates in the evening at the station, but I called to see how he was doing.

"How's it going, Coach?" I asked.

"In the pink," he said, "but I've hired an assistant to take over for a few weeks."

The next morning I saw my new assistant run onto the track and I literally jumped for Joy. I attempted to grab and hug her. She threw me gently, head over heels onto the lawn. If that wasn't mortifying enough, she beat me shooting baskets, then batted every ball I pitched. Whatever we did, no matter what game, she played flawlessly, making me, a world champion, feel like a novice.

I doubled the number of exercises Socrates had given me. I trained with fierce concentration. I awoke at 4:00 A.M., practiced T'ai Chi until dawn, and ran into the hills before meeting Joy each day. I said nothing about my extra training.

I carried Joy's image with me into my classes and into the gym. I wanted to see her, to hold her; but first, it seemed, I had to catch her. For the present, the most I could hope for was to beat her at her own games.

Two weeks later, I was back running, skipping, and leaping around the track with Socrates, who was back in action. "Must have been a flu," he explained.

"Socrates," I said, sprinting ahead and falling behind, playing tag with him, "you've been pretty closemouthed about your daily habits. I've no idea what you're like when we're not together. Well?"

Grinning at me, he leaped forward about ten feet, then sprinted off around the track. I took off after him, until I was within talking range.

"Are you going to answer me?"

"Nope," he said. The subject was closed.

When we finally finished our stretching and meditation exercises for the morning, Socrates came up to me, put his arm around my shoulders, and said, "Dan, you've been a willing and apt pupil. From now on, you're to arrange your own schedule; do the exercises as needed. I'm going to give you something extra, because you've earned it. I'm going to coach you in gymnastics."

I had to laugh. I couldn't help it. "You're going to coach *me* — in gymnastics? I think you're overreaching yourself this time, Soc." I ran quickly down the turf, and snapped into a roundoff, a back handspring, and a high layout somersault with a double twist.

Socrates walked over to me and said, "I admit it — you're better than I am."

"Hot dog!" I yelled. "I've finally found something I can do that you can't."

"I did notice, though," he added, "that your arms need to stretch more when you set for the twist — oh, and your head is too far back on takeoff."

"Soc, you old bluffer...you're right," I said, realizing that

I had set my head back too far, and my arms did need to stretch more.

"And once we straighten out your technique a bit, we can work on your attitude," he added, with a final twist of his own. "I'll be seeing you in the gym."

"But Socrates, I already have a coach and I don't know if the other gymnasts will take to your wandering around the gymnastics room."

"Oh, I'm sure you'll think of something to tell them."

That afternoon, during our team meeting prior to workout, I told the coach and team that my eccentric grandfather from Chicago was visiting for a couple of weeks and wanted to come watch me. "He's a nice old guy, really spry. Fancies himself quite a coach. If you'd humor him a little — he's not quite playing with a full deck, if you know what I mean — I'm sure he won't disrupt workout too much."

The consensus was favorable. "Oh, by the way," I added. "He likes to be called Marilyn." I could hardly keep a straight face.

"Marilyn?" everyone echoed, laughing.

"Yeah. I know it's kind of bizarre, but you'll understand when you meet him."

"Maybe seeing 'Marilyn' in action will help us understand *you*, Millman. They say it's hereditary." They laughed and started warm-up. Socrates was entering my domain this time. I wondered if he'd like his new nickname.

Today, I had a little surprise planned for the whole team. I'd been holding back in the gym; they had no idea that I'd recovered so fully. I arrived early and walked into the coach's office. He was shuffling through papers scattered on the desk when I spoke.

"Coach," I said, "I want to be in the intersquad competition."

Peering over his glasses he said sympathetically, "You won't be cleared to compete for six months, Dan. After you graduate — for the Olympic trials."

I pulled him aside and whispered, "I'm ready today, now! Been doing some extra work outside the gym."

"Not a chance, Dan. I'm sorry."

The team warmed up together, from event to event, around the small gymnastics room, swinging, tumbling, vaulting, pressing to handstands. I stood on the sidelines, watching.

Then the first event came — floor exercise. Everyone looked pretty good. They were about to move to the next event when I stepped out onto the floor exercise mat and started my routine.

Everything clicked: the double back, a smooth press to handstand, keeping a light rhythm going on the dance elements and turns I'd created, another sky-high tumbling pass, then a final aerial sequence. I landed lightly, under perfect control. I became aware of the whistling and applauding. Sid and Josh looked at one another in amazement. "Where'd the new guy come from?" "Hey, we'll have to sign him up for the team."

Next event. Josh went first on rings, then Sid, Chuck, and Gary. Finally it was my turn. Coach, incredulous after my last routine, just stared. I adjusted my handguards, made sure the tape on my wrists was secure, and jumped up to the rings. Josh stilled my swing, then stepped back. My muscles twitched with anticipation. Inhaling, I pulled up to an inverted hang, then slowly pulled and pressed my body up to an iron cross.

I heard muffled tones of excitement as I swung smoothly down, then up again to a front uprise. I pressed slowly to a handstand with straight arms and straight body. "Well, I'll be damned," Coach said, using the strongest language I'd ever heard him use. Bailing out of the handstand, I did a fast, light giant swing and locked it without a tremor. After a high double somersault dismount, I landed with only a small step. Not a bad job.

And so it went. After completing my final routine, again greeted by hoots and shouts of surprise, I noticed Socrates, sitting quietly in the corner, smiling. He must have seen it all. I waved to him to come over.

"Guys, I'd like to introduce my grandfather." I said, "This is Sid, Tom, Herb, Gary, Joel, Josh. Guys, this is…"

"We're pleased to meet you, Marilyn," they said in chorus. Socrates looked puzzled for the merest moment, then said,

"Hello, I'm glad to meet you, too. I wanted to see what kind of crowd Dan runs around with." They grinned, probably deciding they liked him.

"I hope you don't think it's too strange, my being called Marilyn," he said casually. "My real name is Merrill, but I got stuck with the nickname. Did Dan ever tell you what he was called at home?" he chuckled.

"No," they said eagerly. "What?"

"Well, I'd better not say. I don't want to embarrass him. He can always tell you if he wants to." Socrates, the fox, looked at me and solemnly said, "You don't have to be ashamed of it, Dan."

As they walked off, they said to me, "Bye, Suzette," "Bye, Josephine," "See you later, Geraldine."

"Oh, hell, look what you've started — *Marilyn!*" I headed for the showers.

For the rest of that week, Socrates never took his eyes off me. Occasionally, he'd turn to another gymnast and offer some superb advice, which always seemed to work. I was astonished by his knowledge. Tirelessly patient with everyone else, he was much less so with me. One time I finished my best-ever pommel horse routine and walked over happily to take the tape off my wrists. Soc beckoned me and said, "The routine looked satisfactory, but you did a very sloppy job taking the tape off. Remember, *every-moment* satori."

After high bar, he said, "Dan, you still need to meditate your actions."

"What do you mean, meditate my actions?"

"Meditating an action is different from doing it. To do, there is a doer, a self-conscious 'someone' performing. But when you meditate an action, you've already released attachment to outcomes. There's no 'you' left to do it. In forgetting yourself, you become what you do, so your action is free, spontaneous, without ambition, inhibition, or fear."

On and on it went. He watched every expression on my face, listened to every comment I made.

Some people heard that I was back in shape. Susie came by to watch, bringing with her Michelle and Linda, two new friends. Linda immediately caught my eye. She was a slim red-haired woman with a pretty face behind glasses, wearing a simple dress that suggested pleasing curves. I hoped to see her again.

The next day, after a very disappointing workout when nothing seemed to go well, Socrates called me over to sit with him on a crash pad. "Dan," he said, "you've achieved a high level of skill. You're an expert gymnast."

"Why thank you, Socrates."

"It wasn't a compliment." He turned to face me more directly. "An expert dedicates his life to his training with the purpose of winning competitions. Someday, you may become a master gymnast. The *master* dedicates his training to life."

"I understand that, Soc. You've told me a number..."

"I know you understand it. What I am telling you is that you haven't yet realized it; you don't yet live it. You persist in gloating over a few new physical skills, then mope around if the training doesn't go well one day. But when you begin transcendental training, focusing your best efforts, without attachment to outcomes, you will understand the peaceful warrior's way."

"But if I don't care about outcomes, what's the point?"

"I didn't say you don't care — that isn't realistic — but the House Rules reveal that you can control your efforts, not outcomes. Do your best; let God handle the rest." He added, "I won't be coming into the gym again. From now on, imagine that I'm inside you, watching and correcting every error, no matter how small."

The next few weeks were intense. I'd rise at 6:00 A.M., stretch, then meditate before class. I completed homework quickly and easily. Then I'd sit and just do nothing for about half an hour before workout.

During this period I began seeing Susie's friend Linda. I was attracted to her but had no time or energy to do more than talk with her for a few minutes before or after workout. I thought about her a lot — then about Joy — then about her, between my daily exercises.

The team's confidence and my abilities were building with

each new victory. It was clear to everyone that I had more than recovered. Though gymnastics was no longer the center of my life, it was still an important part, so I did my very best.

Linda and I went out on a few dates and hit it off very well. She came to talk with me about a personal problem one evening and ended up staying the night, a night of intimacy, but within the conditions imposed by my training. I was growing close to her so quickly that it scared me. She was not in my plans. Still, my attraction to her grew.

I felt "unfaithful" to Joy, but I never knew when that enigmatic young woman would appear again, if ever. Joy was the ideal who flitted in and out of my life. Linda was real, warm, loving — and there.

The coach was getting more excited, more careful, and more nervous, as each passing week brought us closer to the 1968 National Collegiate Championships in Tucson, Arizona. If we won this year, it would be a first for the university, and Coach would realize a goal of twenty years' standing.

Soon enough, we were out on the floor for our three-day contest against Southern Illinois University. By the final night of the team championships, Cal and SIU were running neck and neck, in the fiercest race in gymnastics history. With three events still to go, Southern had a three-point lead.

This was a critical point. If we were going to be realistic, we could resign ourselves to a respectable second-place finish. Or we could go for the impossible.

I, for one, was going for the impossible; it felt like my spirit was on the line. I announced to the team, "I didn't make a comeback for nothing. We're going all the way. I can feel it in my bones. Let's do it!" My words were ordinary, but whatever I was feeling — the electricity — generated power in each man on the team.

Like a tidal wave, we began to pick up momentum, speeding faster and more powerfully with each performer. The crowd, almost lethargic before, started to stir with excitement, leaning forward in their seats. Something was going on; everyone could feel it.

Apparently, Southern was feeling our power, too, because

they started to tremble in handstands and bobble on landings. But by the last event of the meet, they still had a full point lead, and the high bar was always a strong event for them.

Finally there were two Cal gymnasts left — Sid and I. The crowd was hushed. Sid walked to the bar, leaped up, and did a routine that made us hold our breath. He ended with the highest double flyaway anyone in that gym had ever seen. The crowd went wild. I was the last man up on our team — the anchor position, the pressure spot.

Southern's last performer did a fine job. They were almost out of reach; but that "almost" was all I needed. I was going to have to do a 9.8 routine just to tie, and I'd never scored even close to that.

Here it was, my final test. My mind was awash with memories: that night of pain when my thighbone was splintered; my vow to recover; the doctor's admonition to forget about gymnastics; Socrates and my continual training; that endless run in the rain, far up into the hills. And I felt a growing power, a wave of fury at all those who said I'd never perform again. My passion turned to icy calm. There, in that moment, my fate and future seemed in balance. My mind cleared. My emotions surged with power. Do or die.

With the spirit and focus I'd learned in that small gas station over the past months, I approached the high bar. There was not a sound in the gym. The moment of silence, the moment of truth.

I chalked up slowly, adjusting my handguards, checking my wrist straps. I stepped forward and saluted the judges. My eyes shone with a simple message as I faced the head judge: "Here comes the best damn routine you ever saw."

I leaped up to the bar and drove my legs upward. From a handstand I began swinging. The only sound in the gym was that of my hands, revolving around the bar, as I vaulted, twisted, released again, and regrasped the shining pipe.

Only movement, nothing else. No oceans, no world, no stars. Only the high bar and one mindless performer — and soon, even they dissolved into a unity of motion.

Adding a move I'd never done in competition before, I continued on, reaching past my limit. Around and around I swung, faster and faster, getting ready for the dismount, a piked double flyaway.

I whipped around the bar, preparing to release and go flying into space, floating and twirling in the hands of a fate that I'd chosen for myself. I kicked and snapped my legs, spun 'round once, then twice, and kicked open, stretching my body for the landing. The moment of truth had arrived.

I made a perfect landing that echoed through the arena. Silence — then pandemonium broke loose. A 9.85: we were champions!

My coach appeared out of nowhere, grabbing my hand and shaking it wildly, refusing to let go in his rapture. My teammates, jumping and screaming, surrounded and hugged me; a few of them had tears in their eyes. Then I heard the applause thundering in the distance, growing louder. We could hardly contain our excitement during the awards ceremony. We celebrated all night, recounting the meet until morning.

Then it was over. A long-awaited goal was accomplished. Only then did I realize that the applause, the scores and victories were not the same anymore. I had changed so much; my search for victory had finally ended.

It was early spring 1968. My college career was drawing to a close. What would follow, I knew not.

I felt numb as I said farewell to my team in Arizona and boarded a jet, heading back to Berkeley, and Socrates — and to Linda. I looked aimlessly at the clouds below, drained of ambition. All these years I had been sustained by an illusion — happiness through victory — and now that illusion was burned to ashes. I was no happier, no more fulfilled, for all my achievements.

Finally I saw through the clouds. I saw that I had never learned how to enjoy life, only how to achieve. All my life I had been busy seeking happiness, not finding it.

I laid my head back on the pillow as the jet started its descent. My eyes misted with tears. I felt I had come to a dead end; I didn't know where to turn.

CHAPTER SIX

PLEASURE BEYOND THE MIND

Carrying my suitcase, I went straight to Linda's apartment. Between kisses I told her about the championship, but said nothing of my disillusion. Then Soc's image appeared — abruptly I told Linda that I had to go somewhere.

"After midnight?"

"Yes. I have...a friend — a guy friend — who works nights. I really have to go." Another kiss, and I was gone.

Still carrying my suitcase, I stepped into the office.

"Moving in?" he asked.

"In, out — I don't know what I'm doing, Socrates."

"Well, you apparently knew what you were doing at the championships. I read the sports page on occasion. Congratulations. You must be very happy."

"You know very well what I'm feeling, Soc."

"I can imagine," he said lightly as he walked into the garage to resurrect an old VW transmission. "You're making progress — right on schedule."

"Delighted to hear it," I answered without enthusiasm. "But on schedule to where?"

"To the gate! To unreasonable happiness! To the one and only goal you've ever had but didn't know it. And now it's time to lose your mind and come to your senses once again."

"Again?" I asked.

"Oh, yes. You once were bathed in brightness, and found pleasure in the simplest things." With that, he took my head in his hands and sent me back to my infancy.

My eyes open wide. They gaze intently at shapes and colors beneath my hands as I crawl on the tiled floor. I touch a rug and it touches me back. Everything is bright and alive.

I grasp a spoon in one tiny hand and bang it against a cup. The clinking noise delights my ears. I yell with power! Then I look up to see a skirt, billowing above me. I'm lifted up, and make cooing sounds. Bathed in my mother's scent, my body relaxes into hers, and I'm filled with bliss.

Some time later. Cool air touches my face as I crawl in a garden. Colorful flowers tower around me, and I'm surrounded by new smells. I tear one and bite it; my mouth is filled with a bitter message. I spit it out.

My mother comes. I hold out my hand to show her a wiggly black thing that tickles my hand. She reaches down and knocks it away. "Nasty spider!" she says. Then she holds a soft thing to my face; it talks to my nose. "Rose," she says, then makes the same noise again. "Rose." I look up at her, then around me, and drift again into the world of scented colors.

I came to lying facedown on Soc's yellow rug. I lifted my head to peer at the legs of his ancient oak desk. But now everything seemed somehow dimmed. "Socrates, I feel half asleep, like I need to douse myself with cold water and wake up. Are you sure that last journey didn't do some damage?"

"No, Dan, the damage was done over the years, in ways you'll soon see."

"That place — my grandfather's garden — it was like the Garden of Eden."

"Yes, it *was* the Garden of Eden. Every infant lives in a bright Garden where everything is sensed directly, without the veils of thought — free of beliefs, interpretation, and judgments.

"You 'fell' from grace when you began thinking, *about* — when you became a namer and a knower. It's not just Adam and Eve, you see, it's all of us. The birth of the mind is the death of the senses — it's not that we eat an apple and get a little sexy!"

"I wish I could go back," I sighed. "It was so bright, so clear, so beautiful."

"What you enjoyed as a child can be yours again. Jesus of Nazareth, one of the Great Warriors, once said that you must become like a little child to enter the Kingdom of Heaven." Socrates paused, then added, "Meet me tomorrow morning at 8 A.M. at the Botanical Gardens. It's time we went on a nature hike."

I awoke after a few hours' sleep, refreshed and excited. Maybe today, maybe tomorrow, I'd discover the secret of the senses. I jogged up into Strawberry Canyon and waited for Soc at the entrance to the gardens. When he arrived we strolled through green acres of every imaginable kind of tree, bush, plant, and flower.

We entered a giant greenhouse. The air was warm and humid, contrasting with the cool morning air outside. Soc pointed to the tropical foliage that towered over us. "As a child, all this would appear before your eyes and ears and touch as if for the first time. But now you've learned names and categories for everything: 'That's good, that's bad, that's a table, that's a chair, that's a car, a house, a flower, dog, cat, chicken, man, woman, sunset, ocean, star.' You've become bored with things because they only exist as names to you. The dry concepts of the mind obscure your direct perception."

Socrates waved his arm in a sweeping gesture, taking in the palms high above our heads that nearly touched the Plexiglas canopy of the geodesic dome. "You now see everything through a veil of associations *about* things, projected over a direct, simple awareness. You've 'seen it all before': it's like watching a movie for the twentieth time. You see only memories of things, so you become bored, trapped in the mind. This is why you have to 'lose your mind' before you can come to your senses."

The next night Socrates was already putting the kettle on when I stepped into the office, carefully removed my shoes, and put them on the mat beneath the couch. With his back still turned, he said, "How about a little contest? You do a stunt, then I'll do a stunt, and we'll see who wins."

"Well, OK, if you really want to." I didn't want to embarrass him, so I just did a one-arm handstand on the desk for a few seconds, then stood on it and did a back somersault off, landing lightly on the carpet.

Socrates shook his head, apparently demoralized. "I thought it might be a close contest, but I can see that it's not going to be."

"I'm sorry, Soc, but after all, you aren't getting any younger, and I am pretty good at this stuff."

"What I meant to say," he grinned, "is that you don't stand a chance."

"What?"

"Here goes," he said. I watched him as he slowly turned around and walked deliberately into the bathroom. I moved toward the front door in case he came running out with a sword again. But he only emerged with his mug. He filled it with water, smiled at me, held the water up as if to toast me, and drank it slowly.

"Well?" I said.

"That's it."

"That's what? You didn't do a thing."

"Ah, but I did. You just don't have the eyes to appreciate my feat. I was feeling a slight toxicity in my kidneys; in a few days, it might have begun to affect my entire body. So before any symptoms could arise, I located the problem and flushed out my kidneys."

I had to laugh. "Soc, you're the greatest con man I've ever met. Admit defeat — you're bluffing."

"I am completely serious. What I've just described did, in fact, take place. It requires sensitivity to internal energies and the voluntary control of a few subtle mechanisms.

"You, on the other hand," he said, rubbing salt in the wound, "are only vaguely aware of what's going on inside that bag of skin. Like a balance beam performer just learning a handstand, you're not yet sensitive enough to detect when you're out of balance, and you can still 'fall' ill. And for all your

gymnastics skills, you've only developed a gross level of awareness, sufficient to perform certain movement patterns but
nothing to write home about."

"You sure take the romance out of a triple somersault,
Soc."

"There is no romance in it; it's a stunt that requires time
and practice to learn. But when you can feel the flow of energies in your body, *then* you'll have your 'romance.' So keep
practicing, Dan. Refine your senses a little more each day;
stretch them, as you would in the gym. Finally, your awareness
will pierce deeply into your body and into the world. Then
you'll think less and feel more. That way you'll enjoy even the
simplest things in life — no longer addicted to achievement or
expensive entertainments. Next time," he laughed, "perhaps
we can have a real competition."

We sat quietly for a while, then went into the garage, where
I helped Soc pull an engine from a VW and take apart another
ailing transmission. When we returned later to the office, I
asked Soc whether he thought rich people are any happier than
"poor stiffs like us."

His response, as usual, shocked me. "As a matter of fact,
Dan, I'm quite wealthy. One must become rich to be happy."
He smiled at my dumbfounded expression, picked up a pen
from his desk, and wrote on a clean white sheet of paper:

$$\text{Happiness} = \frac{\text{Satisfaction}}{\text{Desires}}$$

"You are rich if you have enough money to satisfy all your
desires. So there are two ways to be rich: You earn, inherit,
borrow, beg, or steal enough money to meet all your desires; or,
you cultivate a simple lifestyle of few desires; that way you
always have enough money.

"A peaceful warrior has the insight and discipline to
choose the simple way — to know the difference between needs
and wants. We have few basic needs but endless wants. Full
attention to every moment is my pleasure. Attention costs
no money; your only investment is training. That's another

advantage of being a warrior, Dan — it's cheaper! The secret of happiness, you see, is not found in seeking more, but in developing the capacity to enjoy less."

I felt content, listening to the spell he wove. There were no complications, no pressing searches, no desperate enterprises that had to be done. Socrates revealed to me the treasure trove of simple awareness.

Suddenly he grabbed me under the arms, picked me up, and threw me straight up into the air, so high, my head almost hit the ceiling. When I came down, he slowed my descent, setting me back down on my feet. "Just wanted to make sure I have your attention for this next part. What time is it?"

"Um, it's 2:35."

"Wrong! The time always was, is, and always will be *now! Now* is the time; the time is *now.* Is it clear?"

"Well, yeah, it's clear."

"And where are we?"

"We're in the gas station office — say, didn't we play this game a long time ago?"

"Yes we did, and what you learned is that the only thing you know absolutely is that you are *here,* wherever here may be. From now on, whenever your attention begins to drift off to other times and places, I want you to snap back. Remember, the time is now and the place is here."

Just then, a college student burst into the office, dragging a friend with him. "I couldn't believe it!" he said to his friend, pointing to Socrates, then speaking to him. "I was walking by on the street, when I glanced over here and saw you throw that guy to the ceiling. Who *are* you, anyway?"

It looked as if Socrates was about to blow his cover. He looked at the student blankly, then laughed. "Oh," Soc laughed again, "Oh, that's good! No, we were just exercising to pass the time. Dan here is a gymnast — aren't you, Dan?" I nodded. The student's friend said he remembered me; he'd watched a couple of gymnastics meets. Soc's story began to sound almost credible.

"We have a little trampoline behind the desk there." Socrates went behind the desk, where, to my complete stupefaction, he jumped on the nonexistent mini-trampoline so well I started to believe it was behind the desk. Jumping higher and higher until he could almost reach the ceiling, Soc then bounced lower, bobbing up and down, and finally stopped, bowing. I clapped.

Confused but satisfied, they left. I ran around to the other side of the desk. There was, of course, no trampoline. I laughed hysterically. "Socrates, you're incredible!"

"Yep," he said, never one for false modesty.

By this time the sky was showing the faint light of dawn as Socrates and I got ready to leave. Zipping up my jacket, I felt as if it was a symbolic dawn for me.

Walking home, I thought of the changes that were showing up, not so much on the outside, but on the inside. I felt a new clarity about my path and priorities. I had finally released my expectation that the world should fulfill me; with that, my disappointments had vanished. I would continue to do whatever was necessary to live in the everyday world, of course, but on my own conditions. I was starting to glimpse a profound sense of freedom even as I lived an ordinary life.

My relationship with Socrates had changed, too. For one thing, I had fewer illusions to defend. If he called me a jackass, I could only laugh, because by his standards at least, he was right. And he rarely frightened me anymore.

As I passed Herrick Hospital on my walk home, a hand grasped my shoulder and I slipped instinctively under it, like a cat that didn't want to be patted. Turning, I saw a grinning Socrates.

"Ah, you're not such a nervous fish anymore."

"What are you doing here, Soc?"

"Going for a walk."

"Well, it's great to have you along."

We walked in silence for a block or two, then he asked, "What time is it?"

"Oh, it's about..." Then I caught myself. "...about *now*."

"And where are we?"

"Here."

He said nothing else, and I felt like talking so I told him about my new feelings of freedom, my plans for the future.

"What time is it?" he asked.

"Now," I sighed. "You don't have to keep..."

"Where are we?" he asked innocently.

"Here, but..."

"Understand this above all," he interrupted. "You can do nothing to change the past, and the future will never come exactly as you expect or hope for. There have never been past warriors, nor will there be future ones. The warrior is *here, now.* Your sorrow, your fear and anger, regret and guilt, your envy and plans and cravings live only in the past, or in the future."

"Hold on, Socrates. I distinctly remember being angry in the present."

"Not so," he said. "What you mean is that you *acted* angry in a present moment. Action always happens in the present, because it is an expression of the body, which can only exist in the here and now. But the mind is like a phantom that lives only in the past or future. Its only power over you is to draw your attention out of the present."

I bent over to tie my shoe when I felt something touch my temples.

I finished tying my shoe and stood up, finding myself standing alone in a musty old attic without windows. In the dim light I discerned a couple of old trunks, shaped like vertical coffins, in a corner of the room.

All at once, the hairs on my arms stood up and I felt an icy fear. I could hear no sound but the pounding of my heart. All else was muffled by the stale dead air. Taking a tentative step, I noticed that I was standing within a pentacle, a five-pointed star, painted in brownish red on the floor. I looked closer. The brownish red color was from dried — or drying — blood.

Behind me I heard a growling laugh, so sickening, so horrifying that I had to swallow the rising metallic taste in my mouth. Reflexively, I turned to face a leprous, misshapen beast. It breathed in my face and the sickeningly sweet stench of the long-dead hit me full force.

Its grotesque cheeks pulled back to reveal black fangs. Then it spoke: "Commme to mmeee." I felt impelled to obey, but my instincts held. I stayed put.

It roared with fury. "My children, take him!" The trunks in the corner began moving slowly toward me and opened to reveal loathsome, decaying human corpses, which stepped out and advanced steadily. I gyrated wildly within the pentacle, seeking a place to run, when the attic door opened behind me and a young woman of about nineteen stumbled into the room and fell just outside the pentacle. The door remained ajar, and a shaft of light fell through.

She was beautiful, dressed in white. She moaned, as if hurt, and said in a faraway voice, "Help me, please help me." Her eyes were tearfully pleading, yet held a promise of gratitude, reward, and unquenchable desire.

I looked at the advancing figures. I looked at the woman and at the door.

Then the Feeling came to me: *Stay where you are. The pentacle is the present moment. There, you're safe. The demon and his attendants are the past. The door is the future. Beware.*

Just then, the girl moaned again and rolled over on her back. Her dress slid up one leg, almost to her waist. She reached out to me pleading, tempting, "Help me...."

Drunk with desire, I lunged out of the pentacle.

The woman snarled at me, showing bloodred fangs. The demon and his entourage yelped in triumph and leaped toward me. I dove for the pentacle.

Huddled on the sidewalk, shaking, I looked up at Socrates, who said, "If you're sufficiently rested now, would you like to continue?" Some early morning joggers ran by with amused looks on their faces.

"Do you have to scare me half to death every time you want to make a point?" I stammered.

"Only when it is an important point."

After a few moments' silence I asked sheepishly, "You wouldn't have that girl's phone number, would you?" Socrates slapped his forehead and looked to the heavens.

"I will presume you did get the point of that little melodrama?"

"Yeah. Stay in the present: it's safer. And don't step outside a pentacle for anyone with fangs."

"Right you are," he grinned. "Don't let anybody or anything, least of all your own thoughts, draw you out of the present. Surely you have heard the story of the two monks:

Two monks, one old, one very young, walked along a muddy path in a rain forest, on their way back to a monastery in Japan. They came upon a lovely woman who stood helplessly at the edge of a muddy, fast-flowing stream.

Seeing her predicament, the older monk swept her up in his strong arms and carried her across. She smiled at him, her arms around his neck, until he put her gently down on the other side. Thanking him, she bowed, and the monks continued on their way in silence.

As they neared the monastery gates, the young monk could no longer contain himself. "How could you carry a beautiful woman in your arms? Such behavior does not seem proper for a priest."

The old monk looked at his companion, replying, "I left her back there. Are you still carrying her?"

"Looks like more work ahead." I sighed. "Just when I thought I was getting somewhere."

"Your business is not to 'get somewhere' — it is to be *here*. But you still live mostly in the past or future, except when you're doing a somersault or being badgered by me. *Now* is the time to apply yourself like never before, if you're to have even a chance of finding the gate. It is here, before you; open your eyes, now!"

"But how?"

"Just keep your attention in the present moment, Dan. This is freedom from suffering, from fear, from mind. When thoughts touch the present, they dissolve." He prepared to leave.

"Wait, Socrates. Before you go, tell me — were you the older monk in the story — the one who carried the woman? That sounds like something you would have done."

"Are you still carrying her?" He laughed as he glided away and disappeared around the corner.

I jogged the last few blocks home, took a shower, and fell sound asleep.

When I awoke I went for a walk, continuing to meditate in the way Socrates had suggested, focusing my attention more and more in the present moment. I was awakening to the world and, like a child once again, was coming to my senses. The sky seemed brighter, even in the foggy days of May.

I said nothing to Socrates about Linda, for the same reason I had never told her about Socrates — they were separate parts of my life. Besides, I sensed that Socrates was more interested in my inner training than my worldly relations. And Linda had left the university and moved to Los Angeles to find work.

Classes rolled by smoothly as the weeks went on. My real schoolroom, however, was Strawberry Canyon, where I ran like the wind through the hills, losing track of the distance, racing by jackrabbits. Sometimes I would stop to meditate beneath the trees or just smell the fresh breeze coming off the sparkling San Francisco Bay far below. I would sit for an hour, watching the water's shimmer, or the clouds drifting overhead.

I had been released from all the "important goals" of my past. Now only one remained: the gate. Sometimes even that was forgotten in the gym, when I played ecstatically, soaring high into the air on the trampoline, turning and twisting, floating lazily, then snapping into double somersaults and driving skyward again.

Despite the miles between us, Linda and I phoned each other every day and developed a growing sense of intimacy. Meanwhile, the only time I saw Joy was when she stepped out of the shadows or appeared in a dream — her image would float before my eyes, smiling mischievously, until I wasn't sure of what, or whom, I really wanted.

Then, before I knew it, my last year at the university was drawing to a close. Final exams were just a formality. Writing answers in familiar blue books, I knew my life had changed as I delighted in the smooth blue ink emanating from the point of my pen. Even the lines on the paper seemed a work of art. The ideas just rolled out of my head, unobstructed by tension or concern. Then it was over. I'd finished my university education.

I brought fresh apple juice to the station to celebrate with Socrates. As we sat and sipped, my thoughts again drifted into the future.

"Where are you?" Soc asked. "What time is it?"

"Here. Now. But my present reality is that I need a career. Any advice?"

"Yes. Do what you will. Follow your nose and trust your instincts."

"That's not entirely helpful."

"It doesn't matter what you do, only how well you do it. By the way," he added, "Joy will be visiting this weekend."

"Wonderful! How about us going on a picnic this Saturday? Does 10 A.M. sound good?"

"Fine, we'll meet you here."

I said good night and stepped out into a cool June morning, under sparkling stars. It was about 1:30 A.M. as I turned from the station and walked to the corner. Something made me turn around, and I looked up on the roof. There he was, the vision I'd seen so many months ago, standing very still, a soft light glowing around his body as he looked up into the night. Even though he was sixty feet away and speaking softly, I heard him as if he were next to me. "Dan, come here."

I walked quickly around back in time to see Socrates emerge from the shadows.

"Before you leave tonight there is one final thing you should see." He pointed his two index fingers toward my eyes, and touched me just above the brows. Then he simply stepped away and leaped straight up, landing on the roof. I stood, fascinated, not believing what I'd seen. Soc jumped down, landing with very little sound. "The secret," he grinned, "is very strong ankles."

I rubbed my eyes. "Socrates, was it real? I mean, I saw it, but you touched my eyes first."

"There are no well-defined edges of reality, Dan. The earth isn't solid. It is made of molecules and atoms, tiny universes filled with space. It is a place of mystery, light, and magic, if you only open your eyes."

We said good night.

Saturday finally arrived. I walked into the office and Soc rose from his chair. Then I felt a soft arm wrap around my waist and saw Joy's shadow move next to mine.

"I'm so happy to see you again," I said, hugging her.

Her smile was radiant. "Ooh," she squeaked. "You *are* getting strong. Are you training for the Olympic Games?"

"As a matter of fact," I answered seriously, "I've decided to retire. Gymnastics has taken me as far as it can; it's time to move on." She nodded without comment.

"Well, let's be off," said Socrates, carrying the watermelon he'd brought. I had the sandwiches in my backpack.

Up we rode, into the hills, on a day that couldn't have been more beautiful. After lunch, Soc decided to leave us alone and "go climb a tree."

Later, he climbed down to hear us brainstorming.

"I'm going to write a book someday about my life with Socrates, Joy."

"Maybe they'll make a movie out of it," she said, as Soc listened, standing by the tree.

I was getting enthusiastic now. "And they'll have warrior T-shirts...."

"And warrior soap," Joy cried.

"And warrior decals."

"And bubble gum!"

Socrates had heard enough. Shaking his head, he climbed back up the tree.

We both laughed, rolling in the grass, and I said with practiced casualness, "Hey, why don't we have a little race to the merry-go-round and back?"

"Dan, you must be a glutton for punishment," Joy boasted. "My father was an antelope, my mother a cheetah. My sister is the wind, and..."

"Yeah, and your brothers are a Porsche and a Ferrari." She laughed as she slipped into her sneakers.

"The loser cleans up the garbage," I said.

Doing a perfect imitation of W. C. Fields, Joy said, "There's a sucker born every minute." Then, without warning, she took off. I yelled after her, putting on my shoes, "And I suppose your uncle was Peter Rabbit!" I called up to Socrates, "Be back in a few minutes," and sprinted after Joy, now far ahead, running for the merry-go-round about a mile away.

She was fast, all right — but I was faster, and I knew it. My training had honed me to an edge sharper than I'd ever imagined.

Joy looked back as her arms and legs pumped smoothly, and was surprised — might I say shocked? — to see me running right behind her, breathing easy.

She pushed even harder and looked back again. I was close enough to see beads of perspiration dripping down her soft neck. As I pulled up alongside her, she puffed, "What did you do, hitch a ride on the back of an eagle?"

"Yes," I smiled at her. "One of my cousins." Then I blew her a kiss and took off.

I was already around the merry-go-round and halfway back to the picnic spot when I saw that Joy had fallen a hundred yards behind. It looked like she was pushing hard and getting tired. I felt sorry for her, so I stopped, sat down, and picked a wild mustard flower growing by the path. When she approached me, she slowed down to see me sniffing the flower. I said, "Lovely day, isn't it?"

"You know," she said, "this reminds me of the story of the tortoise — and the hare." With that, she accelerated in a burst of incredible speed.

Surprised, I jumped up and took off after her. Slowly but surely I gained on her, but now we were nearing the edge of the meadow, and she had a good lead. I edged closer and closer until I could hear her sweet panting. Neck and neck, shoulder to shoulder, we raced the last twenty yards. Then she reached out and took my hand; we slowed down, laughing, and fell right on top of the watermelon slices Soc had prepared, sending seeds flying in every direction.

Socrates, back down from his tree, applauded as I slid, face first, into a slice of melon, which smeared all over my cheeks.

Joy looked at me and simpered like a Southern belle, "Why honey, y'all don't need to blush like that. After all, y'all almos' *did* beat lil' ol' me."

My face was dripping wet; I wiped it off and licked the melon juice from my fingers. I answered, "Why honey chile, even a lil' ol' fool could plainly see that I won."

"There's only one fool around here," Soc grumbled, "and he just demolished the melon."

We all laughed, and I turned to Joy with love shining in my eyes. But when I saw how she was staring at me, I stopped laughing. She took my hand and led me to the edge of the meadow, overlooking the rolling green hills of Tilden Park.

"Danny, I have to tell you something. You're very special to me. But from what Socrates says" — she looked back at him as he shook his head slowly from side to side — "your path doesn't seem to be wide enough for me, too — at least that's how it looks right now. And I also have many things I must do."

My heart began to pound as a dark cloud descended. A piece of my life had fallen and shattered. "Well, I won't let you go. I don't care what Socrates, or you, or anyone says."

Joy's eyes filled with tears. "Oh, Danny, I hope that one day...But Socrates has told me that it's best if you forget."

As I gazed one last time into Joy's luminous eyes, Socrates approached me from behind and touched me lightly at the base of my skull. The lights went out, and I immediately forgot I ever knew a woman named Joy.

BOOK THREE

UNREASONABLE HAPPINESS

CHAPTER SEVEN

THE FINAL SEARCH

When my eyes opened, I was lying on my back looking up at the sky.

I must have dozed off. Stretching, I said, "The two of us should get out of the station and picnic more often, don't you think?"

"Yes," he nodded slowly. "Just the two of us."

We collected our gear and walked a mile or so through the wooded hills before catching the bus. All the way down the hill, I had a vague feeling that I'd forgotten to say or do something — or maybe I'd left something behind. By the time the bus reached the lowlands, the feeling had faded.

Before he stepped off the bus, I asked, "Hey, Soc, how about going for a run with me sometime tomorrow?"

"Why wait?" he answered. "Meet me tonight on the bridge over the creek at 11:30. We can go for a midnight run up the trails."

That night the full moon gave a silver sheen to the tops of the weeds and bushes as we started up the trails. But I knew every foot of the five-mile climb and could have run the trails in complete darkness.

After a steep climb on the lower trails, my body was toasty warm. Soon we had reached the connector and started up. What had seemed like a mountain many months ago was now hardly any strain for me. Breathing deeply, I sprinted up and hooted at

Socrates trailing behind, wheezing, clowning around. "Come on, old man — catch me if you can!"

On a long stretch I looked back expecting to see Soc bouncing along. He was nowhere in sight. I stopped, chuckling, suspecting an ambush. Well, I'd let him wait up ahead and wonder where I was. I sat on the edge of a hill and looked out over the bay to the city of San Francisco glittering in the distance.

Then the wind began to whisper. Suddenly I knew that something was terribly wrong. I leaped up and raced back down the trails.

I found Socrates just around the bend, lying facedown on the cold earth. I knelt down quickly, tenderly turning him over and holding him, and put my ear to his chest. His heart was silent. "My God, oh my God," I said as a shrill gust of wind howled up the canyon.

Laying Soc's body down, I put my mouth over his and blew into his lungs; I pumped his chest madly in a growing panic.

Finally I could only murmur softly to him, cradling his head in my hands. "Socrates, don't die — please, Socrates." It had been my idea to run. I remembered how he had fought his way up the connector, wheezing. If only... Too late. I was overcome with anger at the injustice of the world; I felt a rage greater than any I had ever known.

"Noooooooooooo!" I screamed at God, and my anguish echoed down the canyon, sending birds soaring from their nests into the safety of the air.

Socrates would not die — I wouldn't let him. I felt energy surging through my arms, legs, and chest. I would give it all to him. If it meant my life, it was a price I would gladly pay. "Socrates, live, *live!*" I grabbed his chest in my hands, digging my fingers into his ribs. I felt electrified, saw my hands glowing, as I shook him, willing his heart to beat. "Socrates!" I commanded. "Live!"

But there was nothing... nothing. Uncertainty entered my mind and I collapsed. It was over. I sat still, with tears running down my cheeks. "Please," I looked upward, into the silver clouds drifting across the moon. "Please," I said to the God I'd never seen. "Let him live." Finally I stopped struggling, stopped hoping. He was beyond my powers. I had failed him.

Two small rabbits hopped out of the bush to see me gazing down at the lifeless body of an old man, which I held tenderly in my arms.

That's when I felt it — the same Presence I had known many months before. It filled my body. I breathed It; It breathed me. "Please," I said one last time, "take me instead." I meant it. And in that moment, I felt a pulse begin to throb in Soc's neck. Quickly, I put my head against his chest. The strong, rhythmic beat of that old warrior's heart pounded against my ear. I breathed life into him, then, until his chest rose and fell of its own accord.

When Socrates opened his eyes, he saw my face above his, laughing, crying softly with gratitude. And the moonlight bathed us in quicksilver. The rabbits, their fur shining, gazed at us. Then, at the sound of my voice, they retreated into the bush.

"Socrates! You're alive."

"I see that your powers of observation are at their usual razor-sharp keenness," he said weakly. He tried to stand, but he was very shaky and his chest hurt, so I lifted him on my shoulders, firefighter style, and began carrying him up toward the end of the trails, two miles away. From the Lawrence Science Lab, the night watchman could call an ambulance.

He rested quietly on my shoulders most of the way as I fought fatigue, sweating under his weight. Now and then he would say, "The only way to travel — let's do this more often" — or "Giddyup."

I returned home only after he was settled into the intensive care unit at Herrick Hospital. That night the dream returned. Death reached out for Socrates; with a cry, I awoke.

I sat with him during the next day. He was asleep most of the time, but late in the afternoon he wanted to talk.

"OK — what happened?"

"I found you lying there. Your heart had stopped and you weren't breathing. I — I willed you to live."

"Remind me to put you in my will, too. What did you feel?"

"That was the strange part, Soc. At first I felt energy course through me. I tried to give it to you. I had nearly given up, when..."

"Never say die," he proclaimed.

"Socrates, this is serious!"

"Continue — I'm rooting for you. I can't wait to find out how it all came out."

I grinned. "You know damn well how it came out. Your heart started beating again — but only after I stopped trying. The Presence I once felt — *It* started your heartbeat."

He nodded. "You were feeling *It*." It wasn't a question, but a statement.

"Yes."

"That was a good lesson," he said, stretching gently.

"A lesson! You had a heart attack and it was a nice little lesson for me? That's how you see it?"

"Yes," he said. "And I hope you make good use of it. No matter how strong we appear, each of us has a hidden weakness that may be our ultimate undoing. House Rules: For every strength there is a weakness — and for every weakness, a strength. Even as a child, my weakness has always been my heart. And you, my young friend, have another kind of 'heart trouble.'"

"*I* do?"

"Yes. You haven't yet opened your heart fully, to life, to each moment. The peaceful warrior's way is not about invulnerability, but absolute vulnerability — to the world, to life, and to the Presence you felt. All along I've shown you by example that a warrior's life is not about imagined perfection or victory; it is about love. Love is the warrior's sword; wherever it cuts, it gives life, not death."

"Socrates, tell me about love. I want so much to understand."

"Love is not something to be understood; it can only be lived."

I looked down at him, realizing the extent of his sacrifice — how he had trained with me, never holding back, even though he knew he had a heart condition — all, just to keep my interest. My eyes filled with tears. "I do feel, Soc..."

"Bullshit! Sorrow is not good enough."

My shame turned to frustration. "You can be infuriating sometimes, you old wizard! What do you want from me, blood?"

"Anger is not good enough," he intoned dramatically, pointing at me with his eyes popping out like an old-fashioned movie villain.

"Socrates, you are completely loony," I laughed.

"Yes — that's *it* — laughter *is* good enough!"

I laughed with him until, chuckling softly, he fell asleep. I left quietly.

When I came to visit the next morning, he appeared stronger. I took him to task right away. "Socrates, why did you persist in running with me and doing all those leaps and bounds when you knew that they might kill you at any time?"

"Better to live until you die," he said. "I am a warrior, so my way is action. I am a teacher, so I teach by example. Some day you may teach others as I have taught you — then you'll understand that words are not enough; you, too, must teach by example what you've realized through experience."

Then he told me a story:

A mother brought her young son to Mahatma Gandhi. She begged, "Please, Mahatma. Tell my son to stop eating sugar."

Gandhi paused, then said, "Bring your son back in two weeks." Puzzled, the woman thanked him and said that she would do as he had asked.

Two weeks later, she returned with her son. Gandhi looked the youngster in the eye and said, "Stop eating sugar."

Grateful but bewildered, the woman asked, "Why did you tell me to bring him back in two weeks? You could have told him the same thing then."

Gandhi replied, "Two weeks ago, *I* was eating sugar."

"So remember, Dan, embody what you teach, and teach only what you have embodied."

"What would I teach other than gymnastics?"

"Gymnastics is enough for now; use it as a way to convey universal lessons," he said. "Give people what they want until they want what you want to give them. Teach somersaults until someone asks for more."

"How will I know if they want something more?"

"You'll know."

"Socrates, are you sure I'm destined to be a teacher? I don't feel like one."

"You appear to be headed in that direction."

"That brings me to something I've wanted to ask you for a long time — you often seem to read my thoughts or to know my future. Will I someday have these kinds of powers?"

Upon hearing this, Soc reached over and clicked the TV on and started to watch cartoons. I clicked it back off. He turned to me and sighed. "I was hoping you would bypass any fascination with powers. But now that it's come up, we might as well get it out of the way. So what do you want to know?"

"Well, for starters, foretelling the future. You seem to be able to do it sometimes."

"Reading the future is based on a realistic perception of the present. Don't be concerned about seeing the future until you can clearly see the present."

"Well, what about reading other people's minds?" I asked.

Socrates sighed. "First you'd better learn to read your own!"

"*You* seem to be able to read my mind most of the time."

"Your mind is easy to read — it's written all over your face."

I blushed.

"See what I mean?" He laughed, pointing to my rouge complexion. "It doesn't take a magician to read faces; poker players do it all the time."

"But what about *real* powers?"

He sat up in bed and said, "Special powers do in fact exist, Dan. But for the warrior, such things are beside the point. Don't be deluded by shiny baubles. A warrior can rely on the power of love, of kindness, of service — and the power of happiness. You cannot attain happiness; it attains you — but only after you surrender everything else."

Socrates seemed to grow weary. He gazed at me for a moment, as if making a decision. Then he spoke in a voice both gentle and firm, saying the words I had most feared. "You have prepared well, Dan, but you are still trapped — still searching. So be it. You shall search until you tire of it. You are to go away for a while. Seek what you must, and learn what you can. Then we shall see."

My voice quavered with emotion. "How — how long?"

His words jolted me. "Nine or ten years should be sufficient."

Feeling a sudden panic, I said, "I have no place to go, no other place I want to be. Please, let me stay with you."

He closed his eyes, and sighed. "Trust this, my young friend: Your path will guide you; you cannot lose your way."

"But when can I see you again?"

"I'll find you when your search is finished — really finished."

"When I become a warrior?"

"A warrior is not something you become, Dan. It is something you either are, in this moment, or something you are not. The Way itself creates the warrior. And now forget me. Go, and come back radiant."

I had grown to depend so much on his counsel, on his certainty. Trembling, I walked to the door. Then I turned and looked one last time into those shining eyes. "I'll do all that you've asked, Socrates — except one. I'll never forget you."

I walked down the stairs, out into the city streets, and up the winding roads through campus into an uncertain future.

I decided to move back to Los Angeles, my hometown. I took my old Valiant out of storage and spent my last weekend in Berkeley packing for my departure. Thinking of Linda, I walked to the corner phone booth and dialed the number of her new apartment. When I heard her sleepy voice, I knew what I wanted to do.

"Sweetheart, I have a couple of surprises. I'm moving to L.A.; will you fly up to Oakland as soon as you can tomorrow morning? We could drive down south together; there's something we need to talk about."

There was a pause on the other end. "Oh, I'd love to! I'll be on the 8 A.M. plane. "Um" — a longer pause — "What do you want to talk about, Danny?"

"It's something I should ask you in person, but I'll give you a hint: It's about sharing our lives, and about babies, and waking up in the mornings hugging." A longer pause ensued. "Linda?"

Her voice quavered. "Dan — I can't talk now. I'll fly up early tomorrow."

"I'll meet you at the PSA gate. 'Bye, Linda."

"'Bye, Danny." Then there was the lonely buzz on the line.

I arrived at the gate by 8:45 A.M. She was already standing there, bright-eyed, a beauty with dazzling red hair. She ran up to me, laughing, and threw her arms around me. "Ooh, it's good to hold you again, Danny!"

I could feel the warmth of her body radiate into mine. We walked quickly to the parking lot, not finding any words at first.

I drove back up to Tilden Park and turned right, climbing to Inspiration Point. I had it all planned. I asked her to sit on the fence and was about to pop the question, when she threw her arms around me and said, "Yes!" and began to cry. "Was it something I said?" I joked feebly.

We were married in the Los Angeles Municipal Courthouse in a beautiful private ceremony. Part of me felt very happy; another part was unaccountably depressed. I awoke in the middle of the night and gently tiptoed out to the balcony of our honeymoon suite. I cried soundlessly. Why did I feel as if I had lost something, as if I had *forgotten something important?* The feeling was never to leave me.

We soon settled into a new apartment. I tried my hand at selling life insurance; Linda got a part-time job as a bank teller. We were comfortable and settled, but I was too busy to devote much time to my new wife. Late at night, when she was sleeping, I sat in meditation. Early in the morning I would do a few exercises. But before long my job responsibilities left me little time for such things; all my training and discipline began to fade.

After six months of sales work, I had had enough. I sat down with Linda for our first good talk in many weeks.

"Honey, how do you feel about moving back up to northern California and looking for different work?"

"If that's what you want to do, Dan, it's OK with me. Besides, it might be nice to be near my folks. They're great baby-sitters."

"Baby-sitters?"

"Yes. How do you feel about being a father?"

"You mean a baby? You — me — a baby?" I hugged her very gently for a long time.

I couldn't make any wrong moves after that. The second day up north Linda visited her folks and I went job hunting. I learned from my ex-coach Hal that the men's coaching position for gymnastics was open at Stanford University. I interviewed for the job that day and drove up to my in-laws' to tell Linda the news. When I arrived, they said I had received a call from the Stanford athletic director and had been offered the coaching job, to begin in September. I accepted; I'd found a career, just like that.

In late August, our beautiful daughter, Holly, was born. I drove all our belongings up to Menlo Park and moved us into a comfortable apartment. Linda and the baby flew up two weeks later. We were contented, for a time, but I was soon immersed in my job, developing a strong gymnastics program at Stanford. I ran for miles through the golf course early each morning and often sat alone on the shore of Lake Lagunita. Again, my energies and attention flew in many directions, but sadly, not in Linda's.

A year went by almost without my noticing it. Everything was going so well; I couldn't understand my persistent feeling that I had lost something, a long time ago. The sharp images of my training with Socrates — running into the hills, the strange exercises late at night, the hours of talking and listening and watching my enigmatic teacher — were fading memories.

Not long after our first anniversary, Linda told me she wanted us to see a marriage counselor. It came as a complete shock, just when I felt we'd be able to relax and have more time together.

The marriage counselor did help, yet a shadow had come between Linda and me — maybe it had been there since our wedding night. She had grown quiet and private, drawing Holly with her into her own world. I came home from work each day totally spent, with too little energy left for either of them.

My third year at Stanford, I applied for the position of faculty resident in one of the university residence halls so that Linda could be with other people. It soon became apparent that this move had worked only too well, especially in the arena of romance. She had formed her own social life, and I had been relieved of a burden I could not, or would not, fulfill. Linda and I were separated in the spring of my third year at Stanford. I delved even deeper into my work, and began my inner search once again. I sat with a Zen group in the mornings in our gym. I began to study aikido in the evenings. I read more and more, hoping to find some clues or directions or answers to my unfinished business.

When I was offered a faculty position at Oberlin College, a residential liberal arts college in Ohio, it seemed like a second chance for us. But my search for happiness only intensified. I created courses like "Psychophysical Development" and "Way of the Peaceful Warrior" — which shared some of the perspectives and skills I'd learned from Socrates. At the end of my first year, I received a special grant from the college to travel and do research in my chosen field.

That summer, Linda and I separated. Leaving her and my young daughter behind for a time, I set off on what I hoped would be my final search.

I was to visit many places around the world — Hawaii, Japan, Hong Kong, India, and elsewhere, where I encountered extraordinary teachers, and schools of yoga, martial arts, and shamanism. I had many experiences and found great wisdom, but no lasting peace.

As my travels neared their conclusion, I became even more desperate — compelled toward a final confrontation with the questions that rang out in my mind: "What is enlightenment?

When will I find peace?" Socrates had spoken of these things, but at the time, I didn't have the ears to hear him.

When I arrived in the village of Cascais on the coast of Portugal, the last stop on my journey, the questions continued to replay themselves endlessly, burning deeper into my mind.

One morning I awoke on an isolated stretch of beach where I had camped for a few days. My gaze drifted to the water, where the tide was devouring my painstakingly constructed castle of sand and sticks.

For some reason, this reminded me of my own death, and what Socrates had tried to tell me. His words and gestures played back in bits and pieces, like the twigs from my castle, now scattered and floating in the shallow surf: "Consider your fleeting years, Danny. One day you'll discover that death is not what you might imagine; but then, neither is life. Either may be wondrous, filled with change; or, if you do not awaken, both may turn out to be a considerable disappointment."

His laughter rang out in my memory. Then I remembered an incident in the station: I had been acting lethargic; Socrates suddenly grabbed me and shook me. "Wake up! If you knew for certain that you had a terminal illness — if you had little time left to live — you would waste precious little of it! Well, I'm telling you, Dan — you *do* have a terminal illness: It's called birth. You don't have more than a few years left. No one does! So be happy *now*, without reason — or you never will be at all."

I began to feel a terrible sense of urgency, but there was nowhere to go. So I stayed, a beachcomber who never stopped combing through his own mind. "Who am I? What is enlightenment?"

Socrates had told me, long ago, that even for the warrior, there is no victory over death; there is only the realization of Who we all really are.

As I lay in the sun, I remembered peeling away the last layer of the onion in Soc's office to see "who I was." I remembered a character in a J. D. Salinger novel, who, upon seeing someone drink a glass of milk, said, "It was like pouring God into God, if you know what I mean."

I remembered Chuang Tzu's dream:

Chuang Tzu fell asleep and dreamed he was a butterfly. Upon awakening, he asked himself, "Am I a man who has just been dreaming that he was a butterfly, or a sleeping butterfly, now dreaming that he is a man?"

I walked down the beach, singing the children's nursery rhyme over and over:

"Row, row, row your boat, gently down the stream,
Merrily, merrily, merrily, merrily, life is but a dream."

After one afternoon walk, I returned to my sheltered campsite, hidden behind some rocks. I reached into my pack and took out an old book I'd picked up in India. It was a ragged English translation of spiritual folktales. Flipping through the pages, I came upon a story about enlightenment:

"Milarepa had searched everywhere for enlightenment, but could find no answer — until one day, he saw an old man walking slowly down a mountain path, carrying a heavy sack. Immediately, Milarepa sensed that this old man knew the secret he had been desperately seeking for many years.

"'Old man, please tell me what you know. What is enlightenment?'

"The old man smiled at him for a moment, and swung the heavy burden off his shoulders, and stood straight.

"'Yes, I see!' cried Milarepa. 'My everlasting gratitude. But please, one question more. What is *after* enlightenment?'

"Smiling again, the old man picked up the sack once again, slung it over his shoulders, steadied his burden, and continued on his way."

That same night I had a dream:

I am in darkness at the foot of a great mountain, searching under every stone for a precious jewel. The valley is covered in darkness, so I cannot find the jewel.

Then I look up at the shining mountain peak. If the jewel is to be found, it must be at the top. I climb and

climb, beginning an arduous journey that takes many
years. At last I reach my journey's end. I stand bathed
in the bright light.

My eyesight is clear now, yet the jewel is nowhere
to be found. I look upon the valley far below, where I
began the climb many years ago. Only then do I realize
that the jewel had always been within me, even then,
and that the light had always shined. Only my eyes had
been closed.

I awoke in the middle of the night, under a shining moon.
The air was warm and the world was silent, except for the
rhythmic wash of the tides. I heard Soc's voice but knew that it
was only another memory: "Enlightenment is not an attainment, Dan; it is a Realization. And when you wake up, everything changes and nothing changes. If a blind man realizes that
he can see, has the world changed?"

I sat and watched the moonlight sparkling on the sea and
capping the distant mountains with silver. "What was that
saying about mountains, and rivers, and the great search?"
"Ah, yes," I remembered:

"First mountains are mountains and rivers are rivers.

"Then mountains are no longer mountains and rivers are
no longer rivers.

"Finally, mountains are mountains and rivers are rivers."

I stood, ran down the beach, and dove into the dark ocean,
swimming out far beyond the surf. I had stopped to tread
water when I suddenly sensed a creature swimming through
the black depths somewhere below my feet. Something was
coming at me, very rapidly: it was Death.

I flailed wildly to the shore and lay panting on the wet
sand. A small crab crawled in front of my eyes and burrowed
into the sand as a wave washed over it.

I stood, dried myself, and slipped into my clothes. I packed
by the light of the moon. Then, shouldering my knapsack, I
repeated a phrase one teacher had said of the search for
enlightenment:

"Better never begin; once begun, better finish."

I knew it was time to go home.

As the jumbo jet settled onto the runway at Hopkins Airport in Cleveland, I felt a growing anxiety about my marriage and my life. Over six years had passed. I felt older, but no wiser. What could I say to my wife and my daughter? Would I ever see Socrates again — and if I did, what could I bring to him?

Linda and Holly were waiting for me when I got off the plane. Holly ran to me squealing with delight, and hugged me tight. My embrace with Linda was soft and warm, but empty of real intimacy, like hugging an old friend. It was obvious that time and experience had drawn us in different directions. Linda had not been lonely in my absence — she had found new friends and intimacies.

And as it happened, soon after my return to Oberlin I met someone very special: a student, a sweet young woman named Joyce. Her short black hair hung in bangs over a pretty face and bright smile. She was small, and full of life. I felt intensely attracted to her, and we spent every available hour together, walking and talking, strolling through the arboretum grounds, around the placid waters. I was able to talk with her in a way I'd never been able to speak with Linda — not because Linda couldn't understand, but because her paths and interests lay elsewhere.

Joyce graduated in the spring. She wanted to stay near me, but I felt a duty to my marriage, so we sadly parted. I knew I'd never forget her, but my family had to come first.

In the middle of the next winter, Linda, Holly, and I moved back to northern California. Perhaps it was my preoccupation with my work and with myself that was the final blow to our marriage, but no omen had been so sad as the continual nagging doubt and melancholy I first felt on our wedding night — that painful doubt, that sense of something I should remember, something I'd left behind me years ago. Only with Joyce had I felt free of it.

After the divorce, Linda and Holly moved into a fine old

house. I lost myself in my work teaching gymnastics and aikido at the Berkeley YMCA.

The temptation to visit the gas station was agonizing, but I would not go until I was called. Besides, how could I go back? I had nothing at all to show for my years.

I moved to Palo Alto and lived alone, as lonely as I had ever been. I thought of Joyce many times, but knew I had no right to call her; I still had unfinished business.

I began my training anew. I exercised, read, meditated, and continued driving questions deeper and deeper into my mind, like a sword. In a matter of months, I started to feel a renewed sense of well-being that I hadn't felt in years. During this time, I started writing, recording volumes of notes from my days with Socrates. I hoped my review of our time together would give me a fresh clue. Nothing had really changed — at least nothing I could see — since he had sent me away.

One morning, I sat on the front steps of my small apartment, overlooking the freeway. I thought back over the past eight years. I had begun as a fool and had almost become a warrior. Then Socrates had sent me out into the world to learn, and I'd become a fool again.

It seemed a waste — all eight years. So here I sat on the steps, gazing over the city to the mountains beyond. Suddenly my attention narrowed, and the mountains began to take on a soft glow. In that instant, I knew what I would do.

I sold what few belongings I had left, strapped my pack to my back, and hitchhiked south toward Fresno, then headed east into the Sierra Nevada. It was late summer — a good time to get lost in the mountains.

CHAPTER EIGHT

THE GATE OPENS

On a narrow road somewhere near Edison Lake, I started hiking inward to an area Socrates had once mentioned — inward and upward, toward the heart of the wilderness. I sensed that here in the mountains I would find the answer — or die. In a way, I was right on both counts.

I hiked up through alpine meadows, between granite peaks, winding my way through thick groves of pine and spruce, up into the high lake country, where people were scarcer than the puma, deer, and small lizards that scurried under rocks as I approached.

I made camp just before dusk. The next day I climbed higher, across great fields of granite at the edge of the timberline. I climbed over huge boulders, cut through canyons and ravines. In the afternoon I picked edible roots and berries, and lay down by a crystal spring. For the first time in years, it seemed, I was content.

Later in the afternoon, I walked alone in the wilds, down through the shade of tangled forests, heading back to base camp. Then I prepared wood for the evening fire, ate another handful of food, and meditated beneath a towering pine tree, surrendering myself to the mountains. If they had anything to offer me, I was ready to accept it.

After the sky turned black, I sat warming my hands and

face over the crackling fire, when out of the shadows stepped Socrates.

"I was in the neighborhood," he said.

In disbelief and delight, I hugged him and wrestled him to the ground, laughing and getting both of us thoroughly dirty. We brushed ourselves off and sat by the fire. "You look almost the same, old warrior — not a year over a hundred." (He did look older, but his gray-speckled eyes still had their twinkle.)

"You, on the other hand," he grinned, looking me over, "look a lot older, and not much smarter. Tell me, did you learn anything?"

I sighed, staring into the fire. "Well, I learned to make tea." I put a small pot of water on my makeshift grill and prepared the spicy tea, using herbs I'd found on my hike that day. I hadn't been expecting company; I handed him my cup, and poured my tea into a small bowl. Finally the words poured forth. As I spoke, the despair that I'd held for so long at last caved in on me.

"I have nothing to bring you, Socrates. I'm still lost — no closer to the gate than I was when we first met. I've failed you, and life has failed me; life has broken my heart."

He was jubilant. "Yes! Your heart has been broken, Dan — broken open to reveal the gate, shining within. It's the only place you haven't looked. Open your eyes, buffoon — you've almost arrived!"

Confused and frustrated, I could only sit there helplessly.

Soc reassured me. "You're almost ready — you're very close."

I pounced on his words eagerly. "Close to what?"

"To the end." Fear crept up my spine for a moment. I crawled quickly into my sleeping bag, and Socrates unrolled his. My last impression that night was of my teacher's eyes, shining, as if he were looking through me, through the fire, into another world.

In the first direct rays of the morning sun, Socrates was already up, sitting over by a nearby stream. I joined him for a while in silence, tossing pebbles into the running water and listening to the plop. Silent, he turned and watched me closely.

That night, after a carefree day of hiking, swimming, and sunning, Socrates told me that he wanted to hear about everything I could remember feeling since I had seen him. I talked for three days and three nights — I'd exhausted my store of memories. Socrates had hardly spoken the whole time, except to ask a brief question.

Just after the sun had set, he motioned for me to join him by the fire. We sat very still, the old warrior and I, our legs crossed on the soft earth, high in the Sierra Nevada.

"Socrates, all my illusions have died, but there seems nothing left to take their place. You've shown me the futility of searching. But isn't the way of the peaceful warrior a path, a search?"

He laughed and shook me by my shoulders. "After all this time, you finally come up with a juicy question when the answer is right in front of your nose. From the start, I have shown you the way *of* the peaceful warrior, not the way *to* the peaceful warrior. As long as you tread the way, you *are* a warrior. These past eight years you have abandoned your "warriorship" so you could search for it. But the way is *now*; it always has been."

"So what do I do now? Where do I go from here?"

"Who cares?" he yelled gleefully. "A fool is 'happy' when his cravings are satisfied. A warrior is happy without reason. That's what makes happiness the ultimate discipline — above all else I have taught you. Happiness is not just something you feel — it is who you *are*."

As we climbed into our sleeping bags once more, Soc's face shone at me in the red glow of the fire. "Dan," he said softly, "this is the final task I will ever give you, and it goes on forever. Act happy, be happy, without a reason in the world. Then you can love, and do what you will."

I was growing drowsy. As my eyes closed, I said softly, "But Socrates, some things and people are very difficult to love; it seems impossible to always feel happy."

"Feelings change, Dan. Sometimes sorrow, sometimes joy. But beneath it all remember the innate perfection of your life unfolding. That is the secret of unreasonable happiness." With these final words, I slept.

193

Socrates shook me gently awake just after dawn. "We have a long hike ahead," he said. Soon we set off into the high country.

The only sign of Soc's age or susceptible heart was the slowed pace of his climb. Once again I was reminded of my teacher's vulnerability and his sacrifice. I could never again take my time with him for granted. As we climbed higher, I remembered a strange story that I had never understood until now.

A saintly woman was walking along the edge of a cliff. Several hundred feet below her, she saw a dead mother lion, surrounded by crying cubs. Without hesitation, she leaped off the cliff so that they would have something to eat.

Perhaps in another place, another time, Socrates would have done the same thing.

We climbed higher and higher, mostly in silence, through sparsely wooded rocky ground, then up to the peaks above the timberline.

"Socrates, where are we headed?" I asked as we sat for a brief rest.

"We're going to a special mound, a holy place, the highest plateau in many miles. It was a burial site for an early American tribe so small that the history books do not record its existence, but these people lived and worked in solitude and in peace."

"How do you know this?"

"I had ancestors who lived among them. Let's move on now; we must reach the plateau before dark."

At this point I was willing to trust Socrates with anything — yet I had an unsettling feeling that I was in grave danger and that he wasn't telling me something.

The sun was ominously low; Socrates increased his pace. We were breathing hard now, leaping and clambering from one huge boulder to the next, deep in shadow. Socrates disappeared into a crack between two boulders.

I followed him down a narrow tunnel formed by the huge rocks, and out again in the open. "In case you come back alone, you'll need to use this passageway," Socrates told me. "It's the only way in or out." I started to question him, but he silenced me.

The light was fading from the sky when we climbed over a final rise. There below us lay a bowl-shaped depression surrounded by soaring cliffs, now covered in shadow. We headed down into the bowl, straight for a jagged peak.

"Are we near the burial site yet?" I asked nervously.

"We are standing on it," he said, "standing among the ghosts of an ancient people, a tribe of warriors."

The wind began to buffet us, as if to add emphasis to his words. Then came the most eerie sound I'd ever heard — like a human voice, moaning.

"What the hell kind of wind is that?"

Without responding, Socrates stopped before a black hole in the face of the cliff and said, "Let's go in."

My instincts were wildly signaling danger, but Soc had already entered. Clicking my flashlight on, I left the moaning wind behind me and followed his faint light deeper into the cave. The flickering beam of my light showed pits and crevices whose bottoms I couldn't see.

"Soc, I don't like being buried this far back in the mountain." He glared at me. But to my relief he headed out toward the mouth of the cave. Not that it mattered; it was as dark outside as inside. We made camp, and Socrates took a pile of small logs out of his pack. "Thought we might need these," he said. The fire was soon crackling. Our bodies cast bizarre, twisted shadows, dancing wildly on the cave wall in front of us, as the flames consumed the logs.

Pointing to the shadows, Socrates said, "These shadows in the cave are an *essential image* of illusion and reality, of suffering and happiness. Here is an ancient story popularized by Plato:

"There once was a people who lived their entire lives within a Cave of Illusions. After generations, they came to believe that their own shadows, cast upon the walls, were the substance of reality. Only the myths and religious tales spoke of a brighter possibility.

"Obsessed with the shadow play, the people became accustomed to and imprisoned by their dark reality."

I stared at the shadows and felt the heat of the fire upon my back as Socrates continued.

"Throughout history, Dan, there have been blessed exceptions to the prisoners of the Cave. There were those who became tired of the shadow play, who began to doubt it, who were no longer fulfilled by shadows no matter how high they leaped. They became seekers of light. A fortunate few found a guide who prepared them and who took them beyond all illusion into the sunlight."

Captivated by his story, I watched the shadows dance against the granite walls in the yellow light. Soc continued: "All the peoples of the world, Dan, are trapped within the Cave of their own minds. Only those few warriors who see the light, who cut free, surrendering everything, can laugh into eternity. And so will you, my friend."

"It sounds unattainable, Soc — and somehow frightening."

"It is beyond attainment and beyond fear. Once it happens, you will see that it is obvious, simple, ordinary, awake, and happy. It is only reality, beyond the shadows."

We sat in a stillness broken only by the sound of crackling logs. I watched Socrates, who appeared to be waiting for something. I had an uneasy feeling, but the faint light of dawn, revealing the mouth of the cave, revived my spirits.

Then the cave was again shrouded in darkness. Socrates stood quickly and walked to the entrance with me right behind. The air smelled of ozone as we stepped outside. I could feel the static electricity raise the hairs on the back of my neck. Then the thunderstorm struck.

Socrates whirled around to face me. Lightning flashed. A bolt struck one of the cliffs in the distance. "Hurry!" Socrates said, with an urgency I'd not heard before. "There's not much time left — eternity is not far away." In that moment, the

Feeling came to me — the feeling that had never been wrong — and it said, *Beware! Death is stalking.*

Then Socrates spoke again, his voice ominous and strident. "Quickly, back into the cave!" I started to look in my pack for my flashlight, but he barked at me, "Move!"

I retreated into the blackness and pressed against the wall. Hardly breathing, I waited for him to come get me, but he had disappeared.

As I was about to call out to him, I was jarred almost unconscious as something viselike suddenly gripped me behind the neck with crushing force and dragged me back, deeper into the cave. "Socrates!" I screamed. "Socrates!"

The grip on my neck released, but then a far more terrible pain began: my head was being crushed from behind. I screamed, and screamed again. Just before my skull shattered with the maddening pressure, I heard these words — unmistakably the voice of Socrates: "This is your final journey."

With a horrible crack, the pain vanished. I crumpled, and hit the floor of the cavern with a soft thud. Lightning flashed, and in its momentary glare I could see Socrates standing over me, staring down. Then came the sound of thunder from another world. That's when I knew I was dying.

One of my legs hung limp over the edge of a deep hole. Socrates pushed me over the precipice, into the abyss, and I fell, bouncing, smashing against the rocks, down into the bowels of the earth; then, dropping through an opening, I was released by the mountain out into the sunlight, where my shattered body spun downward, finally landing in a heap in a wet green meadow far, far below.

The body was now a broken, twisted piece of meat. Carrion birds, rodents, insects, and worms came to feed on the decomposing flesh that I had once imagined to be "me." Time passed faster and faster. The days flashed by and the sky became a rapid blinking, an alternation of light and darkness, flickering faster and faster into a blur; then the days turned to weeks, and the weeks became months.

The seasons changed, and the remains of the body began to

dissolve into the soil, enriching it. The frozen snows of winter preserved my bones for a moment in time, but as the seasons flashed by in ever more rapid cycles, even the bones became dust. From the nourishment of my body, flowers and trees grew and died in that meadow. Finally even the meadow disappeared.

I had become part of the carrion birds that had feasted on my flesh, part of the insects and rodents, and part of their predators in a great cycle of life and death. I became their ancestors, until ultimately they, too, were returned to the earth.

The Dan Millman who had lived long ago was gone forever, a flashing moment in time — but *I* remained unchanged through all the ages. I was now Myself, the Consciousness that observed all, was all. All my separate parts would continue forever; forever changing, forever new.

I realized now that the Grim Reaper, the Death Dan Millman had so feared, had been his great illusion. And so his life, too, had been an illusion, a problem, nothing more than a humorous incident when Consciousness had forgotten Itself.

While Dan had lived, he had not passed through the gate; he had not realized his true nature; he had lived in mortality and fear, alone.

But *I* knew. If he had only known then what I know now.

I lay on the floor of the cave, smiling. I sat up against the wall then gazed into the darkness, puzzled, but without fear.

My eyes began to adjust, and I saw a white-haired man sitting near me, smiling. Then, from thousands of years away, it all came back, and I felt momentarily saddened by my return to mortal form. Then I realized that it didn't matter — nothing could possibly matter!

This struck me as very funny; everything did, and so I started to laugh. I looked at Socrates; our eyes gleamed ecstatically. I knew that he knew what I knew. I leaped forward and hugged him. We danced around the cavern, laughing wildly at my death.

Afterward, we packed and headed down the mountainside. We cut through the passageway, down through ravines and across fields of boulders toward our base camp.

I didn't speak much, but I laughed often, because every

time I looked around — at the earth, the sky, the sun, the trees, the lakes, the streams — I realized that it was all Me — that no separation existed at all.

All these years Dan Millman had grown up, struggling to "be a somebody." Talk about backward! Dan had been a somebody in a fearful mind and a mortal body.

Well, I thought, now I am playing Dan Millman again, and I might as well get used to it for a few more seconds in eternity, until this, too, passes. But now I know that I am not only the single piece of flesh — and that secret makes all the difference!

There was no way to describe the impact of this knowledge. I was simply awake.

And so I awoke to reality, free of any meaning or any search. What could there possibly be to search for? All of Soc's words had come alive with my death. This was the paradox of it all, the humor of it all, and the great change. All searches, all achievements, all goals, were equally enjoyable, and equally unnecessary.

Energy coursed through my body. I overflowed with happiness and burst with laughter; it was the laugh of an unreasonably happy man.

And so we walked down, past the highest lakes, past the edge of the timberline, and into the thick forest, heading down to the stream where we'd camped two days — or a thousand years — ago.

I had lost all my rules, all my morals, all my fear back there on the mountain. I could no longer be controlled. What punishment could possibly threaten me? Although I had no code of behavior, I sensed what was balanced, appropriate, and loving. I was finally capable of kindness. He had said it; what could be a greater power?

I had lost my mind and fallen into my heart. The gate had finally opened, and I had tumbled through, laughing, because it, too, was a joke. It was a gateless gate, another illusion, another image that Socrates had woven into the fabric of my reality, as he'd promised long ago. I had finally seen what there was to see. The path would continue, without end; but now, it was full of light.

It was turning dark by the time we reached our camp. We made a fire and ate a small meal of dried fruit and sunflower seeds, the last of my stores. Only then, as the firelight flickered against our faces, did Socrates speak.

"You'll lose it, you know."

"Lose what?"

"Your vision. It is rare — only possible through an unlikely set of circumstances — but it is an experience, so you'll lose it."

"Perhaps that's true, Socrates, but who cares?" I laughed. "I've also lost my mind and can't seem to find it anywhere!"

He raised his eyebrows in pleased surprise. "Well, then, it appears that my work with you is complete. My debt is paid."

"Wow!" I grinned. "Do you mean this is graduation day for me?"

"No, Dan, this is graduation day for *me*."

He stood, put his pack on his shoulders, and walked off, melting into the shadows.

It was time to return to the station, where it had all begun. Somehow, I had a feeling that Socrates was already there, waiting for me. At sunrise, I packed my knapsack and started down the mountain.

The trip out of the wilderness took several days. I caught a ride into Fresno, then followed 101 up into San Jose, then back to Palo Alto. It was hard to believe that I'd only left the apartment a few weeks ago, a hopeless "somebody."

I unpacked and drove to Berkeley, arriving in the familiar streets at three in the afternoon, long before Socrates came on duty. I parked up on Piedmont and walked down through campus. School had just begun and students were busy being students. I walked down Telegraph Avenue and watched the shopkeepers playing perfect shopkeepers. Everywhere I visited — the fabric shops, the markets, the movie theaters and massage parlors — everyone was perfectly being what they believed they were.

I walked up University, then along Shattuck, passing through the streets like a happy phantom, the Buddha's ghost. I wanted to whisper in people's ears, "Wake up! Wake up! Soon the person you believe you are will die — so now, wake up and be content with this knowledge: *There is no need to search; achievement leads to nowhere. It makes no difference at all, so just be happy now! Love is the only reality of the world, because it is all One, you see. And the only laws are paradox, humor, and change. There is no problem, never was, and never will be. Release your struggle, let go of your mind, throw away your concerns, and relax into the world. No need to resist life; just do your best. Open your eyes and see that you are far more than you imagine. You are the world, you are the universe; you are yourself and everyone else, too! It's all the marvelous Play of God. Wake up, regain your humor. Don't worry, you are already free!"*

I wanted to say it to everyone I met, but if I had, they might have considered me deranged or even dangerous. I knew the wisdom of silence.

The shops were closing. In a few hours it would be time for Soc's shift at the station. I drove to the hills, left my car, and sat on a cliff overlooking the bay. I looked down upon the city of San Francisco in the distance, and at the Golden Gate. I could feel it all, the birds nestled in their nests in the wooded hills of Marin across the bay. I felt the life of the city, the lovers embracing, the criminals at work, the social volunteers giving what they could. And I knew that all of it, the compassion and cruelty, the high and low, the sacred and profane, were all a perfect part of the Play. Everyone played their roles so well! And I was all of it, every smidgen of it. I gazed to the ends of the world, and loved it all.

I closed my eyes to meditate, but realized that I was always meditating now, with my eyes wide open.

After midnight I drove into the station; the bell clanged my arrival. Out of the warmly lit office came my friend, a man who looked like a robust fifty-year-old: slim, leathery, graceful. He came around to the driver's side, grinning, and said, "Fill 'er up?"

"Happiness is a full tank," I answered, then paused. Where had I seen that saying before? What was it I needed to remember?

While Soc pumped the gas, I did the windows; then I

parked the car behind the station and entered the office for the last time. It was like a holy place for me — an unlikely temple. Tonight the room seemed electrified; something was very definitely up, but I had no idea what.

Socrates reached into his drawer and handed me a large notebook, cracked and dried with age. In it were notes written in a careful, finely wrought hand. "This is my journal — entries of my life, since I was young. It will answer all your unasked questions. It is yours now, a gift. I've given everything I can. Now it's up to you. My work is done, but you have work still to do."

"What could there possibly be left?" I smiled.

"You will write and you will teach. You will live an ordinary life, learning how to remain ordinary in a troubled world to which, in a sense, you no longer belong. Remain ordinary, and you can be useful to others."

Socrates rose from his chair and aligned his mug carefully on the desk, next to mine. I looked at his hand. It was shining, glowing brighter than ever before.

"I'm feeling very strange," he said in a tone of surprise. "I think I have to go."

"Is there anything I can do?" I said, thinking he had an upset stomach.

"No." Gazing into space as if the room and I no longer existed, he walked slowly to the door marked "Private," pushed it open, and stepped inside.

I wondered if he'd be all right. I sensed that our time in the mountains had drained him, yet he was shining now as never before. As usual, Socrates didn't make sense.

I sat there on the couch and watched the door, waiting for his return. I yelled through the door, "Hey, Socrates, you're glowing like a lightning bug tonight. Did you eat an electric eel for dinner? I must have you over for dinner this Christmas; you'd make a wonderful decoration for my tree."

I thought I saw a flash of light under the crack in the door. Well, a blown lightbulb might hasten his business. "Soc, are you going to spend all evening in there? I thought warriors didn't get constipated."

Five minutes passed, then ten. I sat holding his prized journal in my hands. I called him, then called again, but I was answered in silence. Suddenly I knew; it wasn't possible, but I knew it had happened.

I leaped to my feet and ran to the door, pushing it open so hard it struck the tile wall with a metallic clang that echoed hollowly in the empty bathroom. I remembered the flash of light minutes ago. Socrates had walked, glowing, into this bathroom, and disappeared.

I stood there a long time, and I heard the familiar station bell, then a honking horn. I walked outside and mechanically filled the tank, taking the money and giving change out of my own pocket. When I returned to the office, I noticed that I hadn't even put my shoes on. I began to laugh; my laughter became hysterical, then quieted. I sat back on the couch, on the old Mexican blanket now tattered, disintegrating, and looked around the room at the yellow rug, faded with age, at the old walnut desk, and the water cooler. I saw the two mugs — Soc's and mine — still sitting on the desk, and last of all, his empty chair.

Then I spoke to him. Wherever that mischievous old warrior was, I'd have the last word.

"Well, Soc, here I am, between past and future, again, floating between heaven and earth. What can I say to you that would be enough? Thank you, my teacher, my inspiration, my friend. I'll miss you. Farewell."

I left the station for the last time feeling only wonder. I knew that I'd not lost him, not really. It had taken me all these years to see the obvious, that Socrates and I had never been different. All this time, we had been one and the same.

I walked through the tree-lined paths of campus, across the creek, and beyond the shady groves out into the city — continuing on the Way, the way toward home.

EPILOGUE

LAUGHTER IN THE WIND

I'd passed through the gate; seen what there was to see; realized, high on a mountain, my true nature. Yet, like the old man who shouldered his burden and continued on his way, I knew that though everything had changed, nothing had changed.

I was still living an ordinary human life with ordinary human responsibilities. I would have to adapt myself to living a useful life in a world that was offended by one who is no longer interested in any search or problem. An unreasonably happy man, I learned, can grate on people's nerves! There were many occasions when I began to understand and even envy the monks who set up housekeeping in faraway caves. But I had been to my cave. My time for receiving was finished; now it was time for giving.

I moved from Palo Alto to San Francisco and began working as a housepainter. As soon as I was settled into a house, I attended to some unfinished business. I hadn't spoken with Joyce since Oberlin. I found her number in New Jersey and called her.

"Dan, what a surprise! How are you?"

"Very well, Joyce. I've been through a lot recently."

There was a pause on the line. "Uh, how is your daughter — and your wife?"

"Linda and Holly are doing fine. Linda and I were divorced some time ago."

"Dan" — there was another pause — "Why did you call?"

I took a deep breath. "Joyce, I want you to come to California and live with me. I have no doubts at all about you — about us. There's plenty of room here...."

"Dan." Joyce laughed. "You're going much too fast for me! When do you propose this little adjustment should take place?"

"Now, or as soon as you can. Joyce, there's so much to tell you — things I've never told anyone. I've held it in so long. Will you call me as soon as you've decided?"

"Dan, are you sure of this?"

"Yes, believe me, and I'll be waiting here every evening for your call."

About two weeks later, I received a call at 7:15 P.M.

"Joyce!"

"I'm calling from the airport."

"From Newark Airport? You're leaving? You're coming?"

"From San Francisco Airport. I've arrived."

For a moment, I didn't get it. "San Francisco Airport?"

"Yes." She laughed. "You know, that landing strip south of the city? Well? Are you going to meet me, or shall I hitchhike?"

In the days that followed we spent every free moment together. I'd quit my painting job and was teaching in a small gymnastics studio in San Francisco. I told her about my life, much as is written here, and all about Socrates. She listened intently.

"You know, Dan, I get a funny feeling when you tell me about that man — as if I know him."

"Well, anything's possible," I smiled.

"No, really, like I knew him! What I never told you before, Danny, is that I left home just before starting high school."

"Well," I responded, "that's unusual, but not too strange."

"The strange part is that the years between my leaving home and going to Oberlin are a complete blank in my memory. And that's not all. At Oberlin, before you came, I remember having dreams, very strange dreams, about someone like you — and about a white-haired man! And my parents — my parents, Danny..." Her large, luminous eyes opened wide and filled with tears. " ...my parents always called me by my nickname... " I held her shoulders and looked into her eyes. In the next moment, like an electric shock, a place in our memories opened up as she said, " ...my nickname was *Joy.*"

We were married among our friends, in the mountains of California. It was a moment I would have given anything to share with the man who had begun it all, for both of us. Then I remembered the card he had given me — the one I was to use if I ever really needed him. I figured now was the time.

I slipped away for a moment and walked across the road to a small mound of earth overlooking the woods and rolling hills. There was a garden there with a single elm tree, almost hidden among the grape arbors. I reached into my wallet and found the card there among my other papers. It was dog-eared, but still glowing.

Warrior, Inc.
Socrates, Prop.
Specializing in:
Paradox, Humor,
and Change
Emergencies Only!

I held it in both hands and spoke softly. "All right, Socrates, you old wizard. Do your stuff. Come visit us, Soc!" I waited and tried again. Nothing happened. Nothing at all. The wind gusted for a moment — that was all.

My disappointment surprised me. I had held on to a secret hope that he might somehow return. But he wasn't coming; not now, not ever. My hands dropped to my sides, and I looked down at the earth. "Good-bye, Socrates. Good-bye, my friend."

I opened my wallet to slip the card back in, glancing again at its lingering glow. The card had changed. In place of "Emergencies Only!" was a single word, glowing brighter than the rest. It said, "Happiness." His wedding gift.

In that moment, a warm breeze caressed my face, mussed my hair, and a falling leaf slapped my cheek as it floated down from the elm.

I threw my head back, laughing with delight, and looked up through the elm's outstretched branches, into the clouds drifting lazily by. I gazed above the stone fence, out over the houses dotted in the green forest below. The wind gusted again, and a lone bird soared by.

Then I felt the truth of it. Socrates hadn't come, because he had never left. He was only changed. He was the elm above my head; he was the clouds and the bird and the wind. They would always be my teachers, my friends.

Before walking back to my wife, my home, my friends, and my future, I surveyed the world around me. Socrates *was* here. He was everywhere.

Peaceful Warrior — from Book to Screen

An Interview with Dan Millman

Q: Why is the movie titled *Peaceful Warrior*? It's about a gymnast, not a soldier or martial artist. What does it mean to be a peaceful warrior?

A: Socrates once told me, "I call myself a warrior — a peaceful warrior — because the real battles we face are inside us." This is also my experience. The way I teach, expressed through my books and now the film, is that we must learn to live with both courage and love, because it takes courage to live and to love in this world.

I hold in high regard those who serve in the military, in law enforcement, and others who put themselves in harm's way to defend the people and values we cherish. I also admire those who spend years in arduous training in the martial arts as a path of personal and spiritual growth.

Yet I view every human being on planet Earth as a "peaceful warrior in training," engaged in a variety of personal challenges in the school of daily life, learning to face ourselves, and the world, with a peaceful heart and a warrior spirit.

Q: What can you say about the experience of having your book *Way of the Peaceful Warrior* made into a movie?

A: Film adaptations can be a challenge for authors. Moving from the relative solitude of book writing, where I'm the master of my realm and creations, to the collaborative medium of film has provided quite an education. I've learned the value of letting go and getting out of the way when it serves a higher good.

It takes some wrestling between author, director, and producers to make a film that serves both art and commerce. Because of these challenges, it's easy for some authors — particularly those who don't understand the demands of adaptation — to become frustrated. The late novelist and sometimes screenwriter F. Scott Fitzgerald once suggested that authors who want their books to become movies should throw their manuscripts in the direction of Hollywood and run the other way.

But overall my experience has been positive. I've developed immense respect for the skills and dedication of all those involved in the creation of a quality film.

Q: There seem to be a growing number of films involving spiritual themes lately. What qualities make *Peaceful Warrior* a spiritual film?

A: Several recent films with spiritual or metaphysical themes have opened in limited venues such as selected churches or have gone straight to DVD. Other spiritually oriented films such as *Resurrection, The Natural, Field of Dreams, Wings of Desire, Ghost, Phenomenon,* and *The Razor's Edge* — and now *Peaceful Warrior* — are picked up for theatrical distribution and reach a mainstream audience.

Even movies that have no overt metaphysical elements,

like *Schindler's List*, or a sports film such as *Rudy*, might also be called spiritual because they lift our spirits. So we might well ask whether there are spiritual films or simply films that have spiritual moments?

The book *Way of the Peaceful Warrior* has many spiritual moments — incidents that occurred during my college years. The movie also addresses elements, themes, and lessons about life's higher potential. It offers spiritual nourishment for those people interested in integrating body, mind, and spirit. The film also speaks to a growing mainstream audience, to provide a bridge or transition point between flesh and spirit, East and West, conventional reality and transcendental possibilities.

Dan, the young protagonist, represents all those who search for something more, for higher wisdom. A typical student athlete, he parties and has an active social and love life, but later, through the intervention of a spiritual catalyst he named Socrates, discovers universal lessons about living with a peaceful heart and warrior spirit. The film audience, like so many readers of the book, can now join him on this transformative journey.

Q: How did the book end up getting made into a film?

A: Considering how few books become films, it's been close to a miracle that *Way of the Peaceful Warrior* completed the journey from page to screen. Because of the book's spiritual themes and teachings, it was not an easy adaptation. It took a quarter century from publication to production.

Over the years, a number of young actors expressed interest in playing the role of Dan, and I spoke with a studio executive or two, but nothing clicked for me until 1986, when I agreed to option the rights to David Welch, a stuntman-actor and aspiring first-time producer.

David put his money where his heart was and set out to

develop a workable script. As with most films, we had ups and downs over the years, until 2000, when Sobini Films, headed by Mark Amin, took on the project. Mark continued working on the script and finally put together the necessary elements — director, cast, and the rest. The process is truly synchronistic, depending on luck, the timing of actors' availability, and so forth.

In the end, they found an experienced director and a talented cast and crew. The book had not only touched a deep place in Mark Amin but had also impacted the lives of director Victor Salva as well as the principal actors and many of the crew. So it was a labor of love for all involved.

Q: Were you involved in the final script?

A: I wrote an early draft; the producer also hired a number of other screenwriters to rework the script. Director Victor Salva made a strong contribution and a final rewrite before the film went into production. And about ten days before shooting began, he took ten or so pages of material from my original script — a number of lines and some whole scenes — and slipped them seamlessly into the story. All part of the process.

Q: In what ways is the film like the book and in what ways different?

A: The primary difference is that the film covers only part of the book — my college years — yet it manages to capture much of the heart, spirit, and key messages of the book for a new audience. Those who want the whole story can read the book — or wait for the sequel.

Despite the film's condensations, it addresses the dramatic core of the story: the passionate struggles and growing friendship between student and mentor, and the initiation of a young man into a higher wisdom and a larger vision of life.

In any event, filmgoers can now experience the adventure that readers have enjoyed for all these years, and Socrates can reach out to new generations, reminding them of what really matters in life.

Q: What do you think of the casting of Nick Nolte as Socrates?

A: Over the years, the producer and I discussed many possible actors who could play the role. And readers all formed their own mental images of Socrates, the archetypal peaceful warrior. As it turned out, it was a stroke of good fortune that Nick Nolte stepped into the role. First, because he's one of our finest actors; second, because he had a personal connection to the book.

I also gave Nick a copy of my most recent book, *The Journeys of Socrates*, which relates the story of my old mentor, so Nick would understand the character more deeply. His performance reflected this understanding.

One of the biggest challenges in turning a message-filled novel into a film was avoiding any trace of "preaching." Few actors could have pulled off this feat the way Nick did. His voice conveyed a lot of love and hard-earned wisdom; his delivery of universal reminders worked so well. It was one of the joys that my wife and I experienced as we sat alone in the screening room, watching the film for the first time.

Q: How are you like, or unlike, the character of Dan as portrayed in the film?

A: For one thing, Scott Mechlowicz, who so ably portrays me in the film, is taller than me. And he had to do some rigorous physical training to prepare for the role. Also, unlike the character in the film, I didn't get straight As or have quite as active a love life.

Since conflict is the core of drama, the gymnasts in the movie get into arguments, and Dan and the coach also confront each other. In real life, while my teammates, my coach, and I had our moments, we actually got along well most of the time. Oh, and we didn't drink as much beer. (At least I didn't — I won't speak for my teammates.)

But many core experiences and incidents, such as the motorcycle accident, were accurate — except that my leg was shattered even worse than is depicted in the film. Most important, the relationship and lessons learned and higher truths presented all reflect elements of my experience.

Q: Weren't you a world champion on the trampoline? Why is there no trampoline or tumbling in the movie?

A: That was a practical directorial decision based on what stunt doubles were available and what events allowed the best dramatic shots of Scott (as Dan). So the director chose to feature the rings and pommel horse, although we see some shots of a few other events. Besides, I didn't mention the trampoline that much in the book either.

Q: What about the tag line on the movie poster: *There are no ordinary moments?* Did you come up with that?

A: It was a collaborative decision to use that line as a central theme for the film. It was inspired by an incident described in my book and a lesson dramatized in the film. That line also relates to the title of my book *No Ordinary Moments*, which serves as a peaceful warrior's guide to daily life.

Q: Do you have a favorite scene in the film?

A: I have a number of favorite scenes, some where I laughed, some where I was deeply moved — scenes of hope and despair, struggle and triumph. So I can't really single out just one scene. Besides, each reader of the book or viewer of the film will have his or her own favorites, as true and important as any I might choose.

Q: What's next? Will there be any sequels?

A: It's quite possible. I hope so. That will depend on the audience response and how well the film does in the U.S. and overseas. If the film is popular, we are likely to see more of the story unfold. Perhaps there will even be a film based on my newest book, *The Journeys of Socrates*, the odyssey that forged the character and tempered the spirit of my old mentor.

There has never been a film quite like *Peaceful Warrior*. It wouldn't have been made years ago. The time is right. This film and others that may follow offer needed reminders to new audiences and generations. They give hope and inspiration and show us what is possible for the human spirit on our journey to awakening.

ABOUT THE AUTHOR

Dan Millman is a graduate of the University of California at Berkeley, a world trampoline champion, and a member of the Gymnastics Hall of Fame. He served as director of gymnastics at Stanford University and later as professor of physical education at Oberlin College. He has traveled around the world to various schools of martial arts, yoga, and other integrative disciplines.

Dan's numerous books, including *Sacred Journey of the Peaceful Warrior*, *The Life You Were Born to Live*, and *The Laws of Spirit*, have inspired millions of readers in more than twenty languages. His talks and seminars in the United States and abroad have influenced men and women from all walks of life, including leaders in the fields of health, psychology, education, business and finance, politics, entertainment, sports, and the arts. Dan lives with his family in Northern California.

To contact Dan's office, to join his eList, or for information about his books, audios, speaking schedule, and more, visit:

www.peacefulwarrior.com

SACRED JOURNEY

OF THE

PEACEFUL WARRIOR

From the Preface

During my training with Socrates, I was sent away for eight years to assimilate his teachings and prepare myself for the final confrontation described at the end of that book. I wrote little about those years, choosing not to reveal their content until I fully understood what had occurred. They began with personal struggles and broken dreams that sent me on a journey around the world to find myself and to reawaken the vision, purpose, and faith I had found with Socrates, but somehow lost.

Sacred Journey relates the first steps on that journey. It began in 1973. I was twenty-six years old.

From the Prologue

Late at night in the old Texaco service station, Socrates would sometimes mention people or places I might someday visit for my "continuing education."

Once he spoke of a woman shaman in Hawaii; another time he referred to a sacred book of wisdom, somewhere in the desert. He also told of a hidden school for warriors in Japan.

Naturally, these things intrigued me, but when I asked for details he would change the subject, so I was never certain whether the woman, the book, or the school actually existed.

In 1968, just before he sent me away, Socrates again spoke of the woman shaman. "I wrote to her about a year ago, and I mentioned you," he said. "She wrote back — said she might be willing to instruct you. Quite an honor," he added, suggesting that I look her up when the time felt right.

"Well, where do I find her?" I asked.

"She wrote the letter on bank stationery."

"What bank?" I asked.

"I don't recall. Somewhere in Honolulu, I think."

"Can I see the letter?"

"Don't have it anymore."

"Does she have a name?" I asked, exasperated.

"She's had several names. Don't know what she's using right now."

"Well, what does she look like?"

"Hard to say; I haven't seen her in years."

"Socrates, help me out here!"

Socrates glared at me. "Do I look like a travel agent? Just follow your nose; trust your instincts. Find her first; then one thing will lead to the next."

Walking back toward my apartment in the silence of the early morning hours, I thought about what Socrates had told me — and what he hadn't: If I was "ever in the neighborhood," he had said, I *might* want to contact a nameless woman, with no address, who *might* still work at a bank somewhere in Honolulu; then again, she might not. *If* I found her, she *might* have something to teach me, and *might* direct me to the other people and places Socrates had spoken of.

As I lay in bed that night, a part of me wanted to head straight for the airport and catch a plane to Honolulu, but more immediate issues demanded my attention; I was about to compete for the last time in the National Collegiate Gymnastics Championships, then graduate from college and get married — hardly the best time to run off to Hawaii on a wild goose chase. With that decision, I fell asleep — in a sense, for five years. I would soon discover that despite all my training and knowledge, I was not yet prepared for what was to follow as I leaped out of Soc's frying pan and into the fires of daily life.

BOOKS BY DAN MILLMAN

The Peaceful Warrior Series

WAY OF THE PEACEFUL WARRIOR
The story that inspired millions worldwide.

SACRED JOURNEY OF THE PEACEFUL WARRIOR
The adventure continues as Dan meets a woman shaman in a Hawaiian rain forest.

GUIDEBOOKS

THE LAWS OF SPIRIT
A timeless parable revealing laws that change lives.

THE LIFE YOU WERE BORN TO LIVE
An accurate system for clarifying your life purpose.

NO ORDINARY MOMENTS
A complete guide to the peaceful warrior's way.

BODY MIND MASTERY
Developing talent for sports and life.

EVERYDAY ENLIGHTENMENT
The twelve gateways to personal growth.

DIVINE INTERVENTIONS
True stories of mystery and miracles that change lives.

LIVING ON PURPOSE
Straight answers to life's tough questions.

FOR CHILDREN

Beautifully illustrated, award-winning stories of wisdom, magic, and mystery for children 4–10.

SECRET OF THE PEACEFUL WARRIOR
Aided by a brave girl named Joy and a wise old man named Socrates, Danny overcomes his fears with a wonderful secret.

QUEST FOR THE CRYSTAL CASTLE
Danny's journey through a magical forest reveals the power of kindness and every child's ability to overcome life's obstacles.

Available at your local bookstore or by calling (800) 972-6657.

First came the book.
Then the movie.
Now the questions are answered.

WISDOM OF THE
PEACEFUL WARRIOR

A COMPANION TO THE BOOK THAT CHANGES LIVES

DAN MILLMAN

AUTHOR OF THE BESTSELLING
WAY OF THE PEACEFUL WARRIOR

Available in Bookstores Everywhere
ISBN-10: 1-932073-21-3 • **ISBN-13:** 978-1-932073-21-8

NEW WORLD LIBRARY
www.NewWorldLibrary.com

The Way Begins

The first book of the bestselling
Peaceful Warrior saga

THE
JOURNEYS of
SOCRATES

An Adventure

DAN MILLMAN

The long-awaited life story of Socrates

Available in Bookstores Everywhere
ISBN: 0-06-083302-5

HarperSanFrancisco
A Division of HarperCollins *Publishers*
www.harpersf.com

H J Kramer and New World Library are dedicated to
publishing books and audio products
that inspire and challenge us to improve
the quality of our lives and our world.

Our books and audios are available
in bookstores everywhere.
For our catalog, please contact:

H J Kramer/New World Library
14 Pamaron Way
Novato, CA 94949

Phone: (415) 884-2100 or (800) 972-6657
Catalog requests: Ext. 50
Orders: Ext. 52
Fax: (415) 884-2199

Email: escort@newworldlibrary.com
Website: www.newworldlibrary.com